YOUR MESSAGE

Everything You Do or
Say Affects *Your Message*

A guide to business self-assessment .
and the road to self-improvement

by David Kauffman

ISBN-13: 978-0692190111 (Your Message)

ISBN-10: 0692190112

Every Action You Take or Decide Not to Take Will Affect Your Message

A book for business professionals and consumers

TABLE OF CONTENTS

Appendix 1

Appendix 2

This book is dedicated to my wife, who put up with me as I wrote and rewrote this book. To Ben Gelman (my grandfather) and Sidney Kauffman (my father) for teaching me the work ethic needed to become a successful business person, and to all my customers over the years who taught me the importance of understanding that business is about them, not me.

FOREWORD

Have you ever wondered why you've had a better experience working with one business instead of another? Almost 35 years ago I founded BNI˙, (Business Network International), for the same reason this book was written, to solve a problem that businesses were encountering.

I recognized the need for a successful way to generate a referral business and thus, the concept of BNI was born. Back in 1985, business owners and professionals had two options: networking groups that imposed large fines and penalties, or the other extreme, groups that were more like social clubs. I envisioned a need for a networking group that had both structure and accountability, where people could market their business or company in a result driven, cost effective way through the power of word of mouth marketing. BNI was created to meet this need and continues to offer professionals from a variety of industries the opportunity to grow their business, clients, and revenue by building and enhancing relationships, because how people view your business is central to closing those referrals.

I understood there was a gap in the fundamentals regarding networking groups and solved that issue with BNI. David and his process outlined in Your Message fills the knowledge gap business owners need to unravel their public relations issues. Startups and well established businesses often struggle with the same problems. Such difficulties can interfere with the experience your clients will have and may even influence their decision to become your clients.

David has been a business owner for more than 35 years and a BNI leader for more than 18 years. I have known him for the bulk of his career with BNI and have always been impressed by his understanding of people and what they want from a business professional. He has the uncanny ability to understand clients' needs from their unique and personal perspective. His philosophy is based on the concept that people/your clients want the service they expect rather than the service you want to provide them. The business experience should be based on the customer's perception instead of the business owner's, which is one of the basics of Your Message. He works with over 3,000 business each year through BNI, training programs, and public speaking events.

Have you ever considered why people are attracted to one business over another or why your clients don't return to use your business again? This book will help you recognize the why behind their decisions. One can be an excellent electrician but a inferior business professional. Understanding the difference between these two concepts can be the beginning of your growth in customer service, and thus, the most sought after in your specialty. This book will encourage you to think differently and make adjustments and changes to the way you present your business to the world.

Change can be extremely difficult, and even when it is in their best interest, people will always resist that change. Each chapter of this book will allow you to step outside the box, open your mind and gain the ability to appreciate the need for change.

David will help you realize it is never too late to improve the experience your clients have with your business. Ultimately you can create a business environment in which your customers want to refer you to all their associates. I commend you on the wise investment you are making by reading this book, and I wish you all the best as you venture forth in your business endeavors. You will be well equipped with new skills and the vision to put your customers first, which will translate into a more successful and lucrative business.

Ivan Misner, Ph.D.
Founder of BNI
New York Times Best Selling Author

INTRODUCTION

So, the old saying... Which came first, the chicken or the egg? I know it's a corny way to open a book! Which came first, the book and its concepts or the business (Your Business Basics) to help those who are struggling in business? It's hard to tell. In BNI˙ (Business Network International) I have worked with thousands of business people, some were owners, marketing representatives, and some were employees. I started to see trends in many of these businesses and how they were all working in these self created bubbles. They were all wearing dark glasses that prevented them from seeing each other. Too many of them were having issues in the same areas, and these became the chapters of this book.

Attending many networking events over time I started compiling ideas about how I could help businesses that were struggling by teaching the concepts discussed in this book. So, I am not sure which came first, I think they both developed together. Yes, I do realize this idea of development at the same time would not work with the chicken and the egg question.

I want to explain who Dr. Ivan Misner is and why I mention him numerous times in this book. Dr. Ivan Misner is the Founder and Chief Visionary Officer of BNI and an expert in the field of business networking. He has been referred to as the "Father of Modern Networking" by CNN and the "Networking Guru" by *Entrepreneur* magazine. The late J. R. Chick Gallagher was the founder and CEO of BNI, Delaware Valley Regions. I considered them both mentors, they greatly influenced my career in BNI and my knowledge of mastering it's system. They taught me how to help others figure out what they need and how to correct their problems by creating simple solutions.

I became a member of BNI in 2001 as an electrician, then formed a general contracting business, followed by a travel agency. During the mid-eighties I owned an alarm company, and all these businesses were based on customer satisfaction. If your clients are unhappy you have no business. Throughout more than 35 years in business I worked with a multitude of different businesses, and this gave me the ability to create the concepts and solutions explained in this book.

When I had finished the first draft of this book, or maybe it was the fourth, I asked a good friend of mine, who is not in a business owner or sales rep, to read it and give me her evaluation. (Thanks Valerie!) I was surprised when she told me this was a good book for consumers to read, as it gave her a new level of information about the red flags of a poorly run business. She began to think about how businesses treated her, and maybe how they should have treated her if they valued her business.

The path you will walk as you read through each chapter can be difficult. You will need to decide if you are willing to identify the areas that could be better, and create change. Change is never easy. It can be an uphill climb, but once you reach the top your view will be stunning. You will be able to take your business to the next level by increasing customer satisfaction and retention.

"Who wants to make more money?" When I begin presentations on the concepts outlined in this book with that question, the replies are a resounding YES. I tell them they are in the right room. Next question, "who wants to make more money and do less work?" Again, the answer is always a loud YES, I then have to tell them, "Sorry I can't help you there!" Taking your business in a new direction is always hard work. You will need to put effort into adapting to your client's expectations and wishes.

The goal of this book is not to pick apart your business and make you feel uncomfortable, but for you to understand the view from the other side. No, not that other side with the bright light but the view from the customer's vision. The view from which we as business owners and salespeople rarely look.

When you get to the last chapter I hope you will be on the path to increased business and a happier clientele who sing your praises to a new community of customers.

CHAPTER 1

Your Message has a big picture, and your success depends on it

What do people see? How do you sound? How do you communicate your information? What happens when things go wrong? Will the public use your business? If so, will they have a good experience and want to refer you to friends, family, and clients? These are some of the questions all business owners should ask themselves. Always remember, business is about the experience people have with your company.

Questioning every aspect of your business is an excellent way to understand the experience people will have with your company. There is a great question in a book called *Inside the Magic Kingdom*. It asks, "Who's really your competition?". I love this question! In my opinion, it should really make all of us think about to whom we are being compared. This type of question will get you understanding how you and your business are viewed. I have asked many of my clients this question, and their answer is never correct. They will name all the businesses in their industry. Contractors will name other contractors. Lawyers will name other law firms. These, however, are not the correct answers. This question was designed to make us realize it's the total experience people have with you and your company—from the first phone call to the follow up call to ensure the experience meets the client's expectations — that should be our main focus. It should remind us that *Your Message* will be compared to every other encounter your customers have with all businesses, even those that are not your "competition."

If you are starting or are relatively new to a business this book will help get *Your Message* out accurately from the beginning. Hopefully, you will learn how to avoid making the mistakes that could cost you clients, and referrals from those clients.

If you're a more seasoned business person or owner, it may be a wake up call or reminder that your business is not about you; it's all about your clients. When I refer to *Your Message* in each chapter of this book I am asking you to think about that particular part of your business and how you are addressing that subject. Together, the chapters will create a single message of clear communication that will help you give your clients or prospective clients a great experience with your company from the first contact to the final payment.

How many of you take the time to put much thought into how others view your business? Maybe you have a business plan. Most people who have one don't really follow it, and the rest don't think a plan is necessary. But in your plan, do you think about the experience people have with your company, or is it just about numbers? Does it address what happens once you have contact with the clients? I think most people reason that it is their business to create and run in a vacuum, conducting business the way they see fit. After all, whose business is it anyway?

I'm always amazed that people will spend hours getting ready for a first date or thinking what jersey to wear when going to a friend's house to watch a pro football game. You rarely put that much thought, however, into *Your Message*. What are you saying to others, your clients, and how are they receiving it?

This book is all about *Your Message* and what it says to others. If you want to be better than all your competitors you need to focus on clients, potential customers and their responses to you. You should always be speaking to the public from *their* point of view, not yours.

Everything you do affects the perception people have of you and their decision to use your business. Now, I know some of you are thinking, "Who cares about all the small details; the only thing that's important is the big picture." Well if that's you, I think it's best you change your thought process now before you lose clients.

It's so important to think through every detail and carefully plan how *Your Message* is presented to your clients. When it comes down to it, this will determine their view of you and your business.

In the business world, perception is everything. Always remember my perception is my reality. It doesn't really matter what you think. Many large businesses such as retail stores, banks, and all those drug companies that plaster their sales pitch on TV every night have multi-million dollar budgets. The sheer repetition of their messages can change what we believe, and it soon becomes a reality. These companies can tell us what they think our perception of their company should be and that we should view their business through their eyes.

What about the rest of us though? Do we have the money or ability to do the same? Whether people do business with you depends on how they feel about you and *Your Message* and what importance you convey. Their decision to use you, and their perceptions about you, can be influenced by everything you communicate, both verbally and nonverbally. You are being judged 24/7. Social media and the digital age also have a profound effect on how you are viewed. Today's digital world never sleeps. People can look your business up and see your digital profile, *Your Digital Message*, at their convenience. *Your Message* never sleeps; your websites and social media are always available.

This book is designed to level the playing field and help you understand your clients' viewpoints. We will cover how to influence positive change and alter perceptions about your business. The result will be that your client base will not only want to work with your business, but will also sing your praises to their family and friends. You should be fully concerned with engaging in positive interactions with your clients at every juncture of the business process.

There are so many variables to *Your Message* that you will need to consider. Each chapter of this book will show you how to create the best message possible, and how to disseminate *Your Message*. We will explore face to face meetings, networking events, virtual messages and the digital world, i.e. social media, websites, and email.

There are many tools to help get *Your Message* to targeted consumers and prospects. Many people have no idea how others view them, because they never ask. You will need to use every tool in your toolbox, so it's vital to learn the importance of each, and how they work together to build *Your Message*. Equally imperative is when to use them. All the techniques we will discuss can create the type of message that sets you above all others, both inside and outside your field. Each should be mastered to get the best results from your perspective clients.

We will review your website, business card, name badge, brochures, handouts, verbal presentation, body language, dress, emails, and a behavioral assessment tool called disc. Knowing the type of person you are speaking to is key to closing the deal.

We will look at each tool individually first, and then see how they work together to complete *Your New Message*. Throughout this book, we will go back and forth between you and your business. Understand they are one and the same in the eyes of your clients.

CHAPTER 2

What type of person are you speaking to, do you know, does it matter

One of the themes of this book is *Your Message* and how it affects others. Always remember it's not about you, it's always about the person you are speaking to or working with.

The information in this chapter is based on my version of disc assessment. Disc assessment is a behavior assessment tool based on the disc theory. Then original theory began with the elements of fire, earth, air, and water developed by Empodocles in 444 B.C. He began to understand that people had four noticeably different styles. In 400 B.C., Hippocrates added his spin on the theory and redefined the quadrants. In 1921 Carl Gustav added his thoughts to the process. Then in 1928 William Moulton Marston, published a book on the topic. In my opinion he was the first modern psychologist who theorized this. His theory was that all people are made up of the four different behavioral traits. He also theorized that there would be one dominant trait and a mix of the others. Next around 1948, Walter Clark created his theory and it was then developed further into a behavioral assessment tool by psychologist Walter Vernon Clarke. Clarke hypothesized that you are born with a mix of all four traits, and throughout your life these traits do not change. The system was again updated around 1970 by John Geier. I think it is important to understand the basic history of how this system was developed. I also find it fascinating that this was around in 400B.C.

I honestly believe you can work on your understanding of your personal characteristics and how others view them. I also believe that though you cannot permanently change these characteristics, you can adapt and be able to control how others see you. You can change your disc profile, but only on the surface. Deep down they will still be as they were when you were born.

The disc profile is simply a tool to identify the order of behavioral traits in people. If you take the disc test, you'll be asked to complete a series of questions. These questions will produce a detailed report about your personality.

There are many names for the four traits. The original names were Dominance (D), Inducement (I), Submission (S), and Compliance (C). Later in the chapter, we will dive into them in detail as I see them: Dominant (D), Influencer (I), Supporter (S), Calculator (C).

Have you ever had a conversation with a potential client when you were discussing something, maybe how the job was going to be performed, and it just felt wrong? Not because the content was off, but the connection between you and the client was. They might not be hearing you, or even listening to you. It might be you were speaking your style and not theirs.

When I first became a director in BNI my primary traits came roaring out as I visited each of my chapters attempting to help members get to the next level. A chapter is a group of business people composed of many types of businesses. Only one person per profession is permitted in each chapter; one real estate agent, banker, general contractor and so on. Chapters can range in size from 25 members to over 100. There are many chapters, all at different stages of development in their chapter life cycles.

I would say my personality traits likely were present before I became a director. Four months into my membership with BNI I stepped up to become my chapter's vice president, and three months later I became president and held that position for four years. I believe this is because I am such a high "I" and "D" combination. I always want to run the show.

BNI is the world's largest referral based word of mouth marketing organization. It's based on "what goes around comes around." If I freely give business to you, in return, you will give business back to me. It is so successful because of the policies and procedures (the system) developed by its members over the past 33 years of weekly chapter meetings. I knew from experience that if they followed the system, every chapter would grow and flourish.

So, I went to my chapters telling the members to follow the rules. I gave no explanation of why it was important or how it would benefit them. I told them to just do it because it's a rule and you need to follow every rule no matter what you think or how you feel. For the longest time I did this, until one day a leadership team member informed me that the members were afraid of me, and often would stay home when I was attending. I was shocked, and a bit hurt! All I wanted to do was help.

I called a few other members in my chapters, and they all told me the same thing, we fear you. What was the issue? What I was saying was true. Follow the rules and the system works! Looking back at that time

I can see there were a few things I was doing wrong. Number one, chapters are made up of all types of people; some were like me and loved my style, others were more nurturing and hated my style. Still, others might have liked my style if I had approached it from the systematical or analytical approach. The second issue is that I never explained why they should follow the rules. I just told them what to do and that they should do it simply because it was in the manuals.

Over the next round of chapter visits, I came with a large bag of candy and played games with the members to get my point across. I asked fundamental questions about the policies and procedures, and when they had the correct answers I gave them candy. I began to explain the whys behind the policies and procedures. The members said it was great that I was softening. Not really, I was just adapting. It took years for me to understand who my clients were and to be able to adjust to THEIR styles.

A few years later at the BNI International Conference in 2010, I took a course offered by The Referral Institute. We walked into a room with chairs set up in a "U" shape. Looking into the room from the open side of the "U" there were four groups of chairs. No one really gave it much thought. Those of us who liked to sit in the back did, and those who wanted the front selected those seats.

I will spare you the long story, but we took the disc test and graded it. The moderator asked us to stand and move to the front. She told all the high "D"s to move to the right, followed by the "I"s, "C"s to their left and finally the high "S"s to the far left. Everyone in the room was surprised since they had set up the correct number of seats for each trait. Only four out of one hundred seats were in the wrong group.

If you take one hundred people, the disc system can predict the average of each trait in a set number of individuals. This system changed the way I would interact with people in my business and personal life. It changed my message.

I continue to work to modify my behavior traits and will most likely be working at it for the rest of my life. It's funny, when I look back ten years, even before I knew what disc was, I realized I needed to change the way I spoke to people. Members still come up to me after meetings and tell me how much they enjoy how I speak and present today vs. years ago. It's not so much that I have changed, but rather that I have now mastered my disc and modified my message. Ask people close to me, and they will tell you I still want to run the show, control everything, and do it my way. I just learned how to manage that part of me.

Let's examine the people you know and the clients you have. Understand that there are basically four types of personalities. There are many different combinations of these four types or traits. We all have one or two dominant traits, followed by two others that are less prominent or obvious in our personalities. You only need to identify the dominant trait in your customers to be able to speak with a clean, precise message that will be understood. More importantly, people will feel comfortable doing business with you.

So, if you want to learn more about your disc make up there are many online tests, however, I recommend you find a location with someone who can explain your results in person. If you take it with a company like Asentiv (formerly The Referral Institute), you will get not only the test but also an instructor to explain the system and show you how to use the results in your business. Having an instructor is important; you will better learn how to match or adapt to your clients' styles. But first, you need to understand yourself.

When you think of how you act in the business setting or at home, what comes to mind?

Do you need to take charge of everything around you?

Do you like to follow a proven system, and when you do, does it feel right?

Are you the type of person who really cares about others and wants to fix everything and make everyone feel comfortable?

Do you like to be the life of the party, and are you always the one doing the talking when in a social setting?

These types of questions will help you understand where you fit into the disc system and which personality trait is your most dominant. The rest of this chapter will give you a better feel for who you are. Write down your answers so you can refer to them while you read.

Once you understand your own profile, it's time to look at what type of person you are speaking to. This is imperative. Do you know what type of potential client they are or will be? I don't mean good or bad; that's like asking a lawyer, "What kind of lawyer are you?" The answer will be something like, "I am excellent," or "the best!" Although that may be true, I was really asking what type of law you practice; business, family or estate planning law? You really need to understand personality traits of individuals you are communicating with and what each is looking for in you. Once you understand these traits and mirror them you have a much greater chance of securing and keeping each as a client. You will have taken a major step toward using your clients' perception of your value or *Your Message* to close the deal.

Understanding the type of person one is helps you determine what kind of client he or she might be and how you should speak to and treat him or her in order to retain each as your customer. Most people will respond better when *Your Message* is communicated to them in the format they are hardwired to receive, not the way you want to present it. People like to be treated in a way they understand and feel comfortable with. They like to hear information in a language they comprehend. Understanding who they are and communicating in that same fashion is the key to their responding well to the conversation. You must respect their traits.

Another way to think about this method of dealing with people is called mirroring. Mirroring also involves understanding a person's style and reproducing it back to him or her. You will need to include speech and mannerisms. The key is knowing the person you are speaking to and how you can profit from this theory of mirroring. If you can understand what order their traits are in and how to interact with them, you can make your response match their comfort zone. In other words, when speaking to someone who is a high C, you need to explain your process or how you are going to perform the service.

There is part of each person that is dominant, fun loving, analytical, and nurturing. In the following you will find descriptions of the four traits. Read through them and see where you fit in. Then think of someone you are very close to, such as a partner or family member you know well. What trait is his or her strongest?

D - Dominators: This person needs to take charge of every situation.

They want you to do it their way and so should everyone else, just because they said so.

They state their opinion as fact.

They expect you to listen to them but will interrupt you to voice their viewpoint.

They are very opinionated and to the point.

They are very impatient.

They are tough, competitive, and demanding.

They never shy away from conflict.

I - Inspirers: This type of client wants to lead the party.

They are very social.

They love being around others.

They are very animated.

They can be inspiring to others.

They tend to be emotional, spontaneous, and optimistic.

They avoid conflict.

They talk a lot.

S - Supporters: This type of client is caring and just wants to help solve the problem or make you feel good.

They are warm and fuzzy.

They are mothering.

They usually are quick to volunteer.

They are supportive of others.

They are accepting of others.

They are reliable, loyal, and accommodating.

They like to be around others.

C - Calculators: This type of client needs to understand and analyzes the system.

They are detail orientated.

They do not express a lot of emotion.

They need everything to be factual; no guessing.

They can be a bit of a perfectionist.

They like to see things in writing.

They are logical, controlled, and systematic.

They are generally quiet and soft spoken.

Try to develop a few questions that will clarify personality types. The questions are up to you, and you will need to assemble your personal list. Here are a few examples.

1. Do you like to follow a proven system that includes a clear set of guidelines? If the answer to this is. "Oh yes," then you are most likely predominantly a Calculator.
2. Do you usually tell your employees what to do with no need to explain the "why" behind your command? If so, then you are probably a Dominator.
3. Do you always want to help or solve issues for both friends and clients? If so, you may be a Supporter.
4. If there is a group at a social gathering or party, do you like to be the one telling the story? If this is the case, you are most likely an Inspirer.

So now you should have a basic idea of how this works. Next, think about how to make your prospective clients hear and understand

Your Message. As discussed, most people will respond better when *Your Message* is communicated to them in the style that best matches their personal traits.

Ok so if you decide that the client is very analytical, do not speak to that person in the Dominator style. Instead, explain the process step by step, so he or she feels comfortable.

If the client nurturing, then you need to be nurturing. The better you are at figuring this out, the better you will be at converting a prospect into a client. As already discussed this action is referred to as mirroring behavior.

There are many books and tons of online information on this subject. For those of you who think this process is new, look up disc. I have taken a few courses on it and have learned that with time and practice you can even begin to figure out who you are speaking to just by a handshake. An excellent book on the subject at the most basic level is *Taking Flight! Master the disc Styles to Transform Your Career, Your Relationships...Your Life*, by Merrick Rosenberg and Daniel Silvert.

Action Items

- ✓ Think about what type of person you are.
- ✓ Review the list of traits in this chapter.
- ✓ Over the next few days really think about everyone you see regularly. What types of people are they? How should you speak to them?

CHAPTER 3

How do you sound, and are you being heard

What does *Your Message* sound like on your electronic devices? What does the public hear? When clients or potential clients hear *Your Message*, what do they think? Your voicemail greeting, and automatic email replies reflect *Your Message*. What does it say about you as a business person? Think about this from the view of those who hear or receive it, do you sound like someone they would like to do business with? Is your speech clear and easy to understand? Are you using words and terms everyone will feel comfortable hearing? Does your voicemail recording reflect the current date and time? When you are speaking to someone on the phone or face to face, do you interrupt before he or she is finished? Listening is a crucial part of speaking.

I make hundreds of calls a week. I am continuously leaving messages on the business and personal voicemails of business owners. Some messages are difficult to understand because they are garbled or have background noise. Others take so much time to get through and are exceedingly wordy! Your recorded greetings are not the place to discuss email address, fax number, instructions on how to send the fax, cell number, office number, office address, or other long winded information no one really cares about initially. Each just wants to leave a message.

I asked many people, and they all agree the all time worst possible greetings are the ones that make us feel like you are doing us all a favor by allowing us to leave you a message. "Please leave me a message, and I will return your call at <u>my</u> earliest convenience." Really? <u>Your</u> earliest convenience. Your clients want someone who is anxious for their business and will call back ASAP, because that's the priority.

One of the best greetings I have encountered was, "Thank you for calling; I apologize that I cannot take your call. Please leave me a message, and I will return it promptly." What's the message that will make your clients feel comfortable and wanted? I know some of you are reading this and thinking you should never apologize for being busy. It's ok; it's not about you, it's about clients and their perception of you.

What do you think about the offices you call that have a prerecorded directory system? "Please listen to the following lists and then select the number." Is it easy to find someone in these systems? Do I need to try to spell out the first three letters of someone's last name? Will I want to give up before I search for your name? These businesses need to find a system that is straightforward and user friendly for the public, since this also affects *Your Message.*

Have you called a business where the first thing you encounter is miserable office staff who have no vested interest in the message they put out to the community? I love my primary doctor; I have used him for years. I think he is excellent, caring, helpful, and pleasant. He will spend as much time with me as I feel necessary and never rushes out to get to the next patient. Almost every time I encounter his front office staff, however, I want to find a different doctor.

How does this effect his message? His staff always gives me a hard time. When I ask if I might speak to him, their answer is, "not unless you first have a check up." Really? If I were to come in for an appointment, there would be no need to speak to him on the phone! Not one of them is ever polite. When I asked the doc about it, his reply was "I know, it is hard to find excellent staff!"

Think about the people who leave outdated messages for their voicemail greetings: "I will be out of the office from August 3rd until August 10th," but it is now December 1st! What is their message telling you?

What about those who forget to empty their voicemails, and when you try to leave a message you hear, "The mailbox you are trying to reach is full, please try again." Another issue is the person who hasn't taken the time to set up their message. "I am sorry, but the person you have called has not yet set up their voice mail, please try again." These two messages, either the mailbox is not set up or the mailbox is full, are instant death to your credibility. When I encounter either of these situations, I wonder how many customers or potential customers will not be able to leave their messages and will never call back. These are a direct reflection on *Your Message*.

The solution to the issue of filled voicemail boxes is simple; make sure you answer messages daily and then delete them. Think of it from the customer's viewpoint. Never allow your voicemail to become full. If you are going to leave a date in your voicemail message, make sure it's current. Keep it simple and easy for the customer to understand. I recommend you call yourself and listen to how you sound on the recording. Oh, and don't forget to return those calls quickly!

Remember how all these small issues reflect to the larger picture that is *Your Message*. Your voicemail greeting is part of the overall customer experience. There is an excellent book on customer experience titled, *Inside the Magic Kingdom*, by Tom Connellan. Tom discusses how people compare your business to others. One of the best, eye opening chapters is on identifying your competition or biggest competitor. You will need to read the book to truly understand this concept. (Chapter 3) When I listen to voicemail greetings, I always think of that book.

An important part of *Your Message* is becoming a good listener. Listening is a major part of communication. When I first became a director in BNI, I began to hear the same questions over and over again. I knew the questions that were going to be asked because they would be the same questions every day, day in and day out. Why would I need to waste my valuable time listening to the entire question? The answer is because it is important to the client who is speaking. How simple!

After I began to get to know my members and they felt comfortable with me, I started to hear similar stories about the director I had replaced. Statements like, "I like that you really listen to what I am saying; the director before would cut me off when I was only a few words into my question." So, you can see how important it is to be a good listener. I know it will be hard at first, but stop, listen, then listen some more. You might even repeat it back, so they know you were listening, and then reply. Your clients will thank you.

Listening to your customers and potential customers denotes respect for them. If people are speaking to you, let customers get their complete thought out, before you speak. Listening can be one of hardest things to do. It is not unusual to find yourself interrupting before someone finishes speaking. It takes a lot of control on your part, but once you can master this, it becomes another tool in your toolbox.

Now think about all the clients that hear your voicemail. Your voicemail greeting should be short enough that you do not lose your client before it ends. Fix the phone directory systems that make your callers go through 10 steps to get to you. Train or replace the gatekeepers or office staff that treat your clients poorly. Listen to and delete your voicemail every day. If you get a new phone, set up the voicemail immediately. Update any dated message on all your devices. Call your phone and your office as a client would and listen to what the client hears.

Listen because people want to be heard. Let them finish before you speak. Remember, how do you sound? How do you listen and treat your clients? How does *Your Message* sound to others?

Action Items

- ✓ Call your phones, office, cell, and your home and listen. What is the message?
- ✓ Have someone call your office and listen in on the call. What did you hear? Was your front desk staff warm and understanding?

CHAPTER 4

What you hand out

A vital part of *Your Message* is everything you hand out. Your business card, brochures, letters, postcards, mailers, estimates, contracts, and basically anything you hand or mail to a client or potential customers reflects *Your Message*. The issue is again to whom are you speaking? Most of us talk to ourselves, not to our clients or future clients.

I have seen a ton of dreadful business cards. Massive logos I really don't care about take up most of the front of the card, and some have minuscule print. Why should I need to put on my reading glasses to read your name or contact information? Some of the cards I see even convey the nature of the business. There are brochures or business cards designed by a corporate office or a supplier. You get these for free, but you need to stamp your name on or put a sticker in the white box, so recipients know it was from you. These handouts scream *Your Message* is CHEAP. Brochures or handouts that are not current in formatting can affect *Your Message*. Are they creative and eye catching? Do your pictures, if there are any, reflect diversity?

Your contracts also demonstrate *Your Message*. Be clear about the terms and how they could be interpreted by your clients., What service or product will you provide? What must clients do as their part of the agreement? Think about your timeline. Is it clear in the contract? Do you clarify when it will start and end? What if either side is not happy with the process; is it easy to terminate the contract? All these details should be considered before a contract is given to a client and/or signed. Think about all the possibilities before you even consider handing it to the customer. Will customers truly understand the terms of the contract? What if something changes? Do you have a clause for that too?

Estimates can also impact *Your Message*. Do they clearly spell out the work you have committed to complete? Do they list any issues that may arise from the work you will be performing? Suppose you are providing the services of an electrician. If you are going to install recessed lights in a living room, will there be any damage from installing the wires from light to light? If so what will be done? Does it include patching? Will the patch be ready for paint? Will you have it painted? All this information should be spelled out in the estimate to protect *Your Message,* and therefore your reputation.

Let's return to your most used handout, your business card. Have you spent more than a few minutes thinking about it? Did you concentrate on color and font? Did you spend money on a great logo? I hate to be the bearer of bad tidings, but to tell you the truth the only one who cares about your logo is you. If you hand me your card will I know what kind of service you provide? What's missing from most business cards, brochures, and other handouts is the thought process that should go into the creation of these materials. Most people don't give this process nearly the amount of time they should.

Let's just concentrate on our cards for now, and we will tie it back to the other materials later. Consider thinking through every aspect of your card, every line, every word. In everything you decide, ask yourself WHY you want it or not want it on your card. Also, please, always think in terms of your clients or prospective clients, the people to whom you give your card, the people with whom you want to do business. Look at things through their eyes, since they are the ones you want to grab. Think in terms of what interests them. You are not your audience. They are. Let's go through the process to create a significant and meaningful business card together.

What is the objective of the card? What do you want it to accomplish? What action do you want taken because of this card? Call a phone number? Stop in your store or business location? Visit your website? Think about what you want the card to accomplish for you. Think about the front and the back of the card. You have two sides with which to work. Your card can do many things. It can do more than just offer your contact info. How about considering things like using it to be a mini sales brochure; explain to your clients and prospective clients what you do; tell your prospects how what you do will benefit them. Tell them why they should do business with you. Enhance *Your Message*. Show photos of your people, your products, your place of business.

What do you want to say and show on the front? Think in terms of what is essential. and what is not. Not everything is crucial, so list in order of importance. Let's emphasize the critical items and downplay or not even mention what is less vital or not necessary at all.

Company name: Think about how you want your business name on your business card. Do you want the LLC or Inc. with the name? Again, why does it matter to your clients?

Think about a tag line under your company name that defines and makes clear what your business does. This is important! On many cards I see, there is no indication of what the business does. Don't make that mistake. Let people know exactly what you do.

Your logo: Do you have a logo? If you do, you should use it. But don't get wrapped up on creating a logo just for your card. In most cases, you care a lot more about your logo than customers do. Same goes for your mission statement. It most likely has a lot of meaning to you, but what about them? The only reason to include it is if it has a social meaning the audience you are trying to reach will flock to. Be careful that you don't have a card that appeals to you, but not to the reader. Talk to your clients and prospective clients.

Your name and title: Think about the title you want to present to the recipient of the card. For example, Vice President may make you feel good, but titles like Customer Service Specialist, Your Personal Travel Specialist or Your Mortgage Expert may make them feel good. How do you want your name listed, for example, Bob or Robert (informal or formal) and why? How will people know what to call you? Think about the certifications many people have achieved. Do people care? I know you may, but will they even know what all those letters mean? Leave them off!

Phones: Which phone number do you want them to call? What other phone numbers do you want listed, and why do you want them listed if they are not the ones you want them to call? Too many phone numbers cause confusion. Consider regular business phone, toll free phone number, home phone, home/office phone, direct line (what does that mean, anyway?), cell phone, car phone, fax, pager, etc. The less, the better. Make sure it is clear what callers should do. And remember, all phones listed should not be in the same font size. Make the phone you want called larger or bolder, so it stands out.

Email address; How important is this? These days your email address is as important as your phone number. Display email addresses and websites with upper and lowercase letters, even though you don't have to type them that way. It just makes it easier to read. Consider the following. They all work, but which is easier to read?

YOURBUSINESSBASICS.COM

or

yourbusinessbasics.com

or

YourBusinessBasics.Com

Brick & Mortar Address: Is it necessary to list this? Is it important? If you work from home, do you want your home address listed on your card? Should you have a P.O. Box?

Website: How important is this? How much emphasis should be on your website? It's getting more and more important to not only list your site, but to feature it.

Photo(s): What would you like to highlight? The person whose card it is? The place of business or building, products, services? Things that convey an image? What do you illustrate on your website? Think about the person who is viewing the pictures. Certain industries tend to cling to old pictures. Real estate brokers and travel agents are guilty of this. I always chuckle when I see a card and the portrait photo is from the 70s, and they are now 40 years older, but they can't let go of that youthful picture.

What do you want to say/show on the back? Think about the objectives of the card to get a better handle on what you want the back to accomplish. Notice that I am not even thinking about a one sided card. There are no valid reasons to leave 50% of your card blank. Would you pay for a full page add in a magazine and leave half the page blank?

Think in terms of bullet points, not sentences or paragraphs. A few bullet points are ideal. You can pack more information onto the card, but it may become too busy, or the print becomes so small it cannot be read. Again, what do you want your prospective clients to see? Remember please, that people want to know only one thing, what you can do for them. It sounds selfish, but that's ok. So, let's consider telling them what you can do for them or what's in it for them. Here are some possibilities:

Consider adding some of the items below as briefly as possible:

What you do

How what you do benefits them

Why they should do business with you

Your business features and benefits

What makes you different from your competition

What special things do you do, or do better, or that your competition doesn't do

Make your bullet point lists in order of what is important

Prioritize most important first and move down from there, not by the size of the line

Should you show photos? Of what? Jobs you have done? Projects completed? Feel good/image pictures? This is your chance to say it all in a single picture (remember, a picture is worth a thousand words). Search your files and your website for good photos or images. Be visual. If your products or services are visual, your card should be too. Show them, don't just tell them. They want to see what you have to offer.

Explain what you want them to do, call this number now? Visit our website now? Stop in our store now? This is your "call to action."

Think about the colors you want on the card. Since most cards are on a white background, you don't want a white background. Be different. Look different from all those white cards out there.

Do you want any typefaces or fonts? Just make sure they are easy to read! Readability is crucial. If they can't read it, why have it? Don't use fonts that are "too fancy"; stay away from cursive or fancy font types. They're just hard to read. And make sure the type size is large enough to read easily. Another issue is the use of all capital letters which also makes it difficult to read. Similarly, I should not need to put on my reading glasses to read your name or number. What you see on your computer screen usually looks a lot smaller when you see an actual card. Look at the card on your computer in actual card size. Survey a group of people of all ages to see if they can read your card.

You've just gone through the process of creating a dynamic, creative, selling business card, a mini sales brochure and a useful tool for *Your Message*. Remember this process works for many different marketing tools, not just your cards.

Now look at the other materials you will hand out to potential and existing clients. Get them out and view them from the eyes of a customer. How do they stack up? Remember you can apply many of the same questions here that you would for your most valuable handout, your business card. Remember this is all part of *Your Message*.

Now take out your card and all your marketing materials and take a close look. Spread them out on a table or your desk and examine them. Think about the questions in this chapter. How do they look? To whom are you speaking, your clients and prospective clients or yourself? If you find that your materials are all about you and not your customers, you need to change them and thus, *Your Message*.

Action Items

- ✓ Gather your materials, business cards, brochures, flyers, informational handouts and look them.
- ✓ Can you understand the best way to contact you?
- ✓ Is it easy to find your contact information?
- ✓ Do they speak to you or to your clientele?

CHAPTER 5

How do you look on the web

Remember, and I am sure you have all heard this before, you get one chance to create a first impression, and it happens in the first 7 to 10 seconds. Don't forget, first impressions are almost impossible to change! There are many components to a digital brand, social media, your website, texting, and emails. In this chapter, we will look at your website.

People tend to create their website in the same fashion they create their business card or other collateral pieces. Most websites reflect the individual they represent. The colors and feel, even the font and the information reflect the creator. Most sites are not built for their target market; they are for the ego of the owner. Even when we use a website developer, they will often do what we want, even though there may be a better look or feel for the site. After all, they want the job and will do whatever you ask them to do.

I was on the board of directors of the Delaware County Community Foundation when they asked me to be the head of the Marketing Committee. I agreed and after selecting three others to join me, we began to look at all their marketing materials. Initially we fixed the website. The original creators were all attorneys. Need I paint you a picture? It was all in shades of grey and brown. There were no pictures, just page after page of text. When you did click on a tab, it came in the form of a text filled PDF file pop up. Now, I guess it spoke to lawyers, however, the target market was the local community. We decided to start over. We added bright colors, pictures of people in the community, clean drop down boxes with many more options to eliminate the wall to wall text. We created a site for our clients, not the board.

The information contained on the pages of your website is a crucial part of *Your Message*. Often, business websites are focused on what the owner thinks is important to the public, such as their logo, pictures that have special meaning to them but may be obscure to the prospective clients. Who will your website attract and why? Will they stay on your site, or will they continue to surf the web looking for a website that speaks to them?

I was with one of my clients, and she was so excited to show me a website of a very successful person in her field. We typed in the address, and we looked through her website. To me, it felt like I was watching an old poorly created cartoon. It was so flashy with over the top colors, and things were always moving. There were child like shapes to make it look like it was hand drawn. It had loud music that changed with every page. It was not for me, however; I was not this person's target market. Her message was not aimed at me or my generation.

We also looked at another website from another successful business in the same industry; it was perfect for me, it was straight forward, nothing flashing, just primary colors, no music, just necessary information. They were both filled with information, and they were both easy to navigate, but my client said the second website, for her, was like reading the full version of *War and Peace*. So, let's look at how your website can affect *Your Message*.

So here we are again, who are you targeting with *Your Message*? You need to make sure it is speaking to your preferred audience, and not to you. While I understand "target marketing", it can also cost you clients if you are too specific. Always remember your website should be able to attract all types of potential customers.

Before you build a website, or if you have a website that was created by a company you hired, make sure you put enough thought into it. Start by making a list of your goals for the website. Do you want to give away some free information as a hook to get visitors to give you their email and build your database? Do you want them to contact you? Do you want to showcase a particular part of your business or product to educate the public about your company? There are many types of websites; what yours should look like depends on your goal.

Is the overall view of *Your Message* clear? I should be able to understand what you do and the object of your website within seconds of opening your home page. It should also have enough in its mix of style to have a general appeal to all types of people. It should feel comforting and informative to all.

What should you consider?

The information on the website should be easy to read; readers should not need to put on their reading glasses because the size of the font is too small. The font itself is sometimes an issue, as some, especially fancy ones, are harder to read than others.

Look at the layout. Most websites have some tabs or buttons. Should they be across the top, down the side, or a combination of both? How large should they be, what color and shape? Are they clear and well marked as to what they will do? If it has a drop down box or list from the tab does the name of the tab reflect what is on the list? Are the tabs easy to use and does the navigation work quickly and correctly? Will it open a new window or just a box on the existing page? There's plenty to think about.

How cluttered does it look? It needs to have enough blank space to make it easy on the eyes.

What colors are best for *Your Message*? Should you have your own pictures or are you using stock pictures? If they are stock pictures will we have seen them on other websites or, worse yet, your competitor's website? AVOID background music! Chances are it will drive people away.

Make sure there are no broken links. If I click on a tab and get a blank page or a message stating "page not found," or the little circle just spins and spins and spins, I will leave your page! What type of reflection will that be on *Your Message*?

What about dated or outdated information? When the information on your website is old or stale, it tells your clients that you don't care about *Your Message,* or it cannot be trusted. It looks like no one is paying attention to the content or the business. So, could I also conclude you will not pay much attention to me if I were your client?

Keeping timely information is imperative if you are blogging on your website. Blogging must be kept current and timely. If you are going to make blogging part of *Your Message*, I would suggest you write at least a dozen blogs ahead of time and keep those posts on file. Every time you post you write another. This way if you get tied up and can't write you will have three months of backup to protect *Your Message*. We will look at this in more detail in the chapter on blogging.

Did you know that 50% of all internet searches originate on a mobile device? When your website is viewed on the many different types of devices how does it look?

Today people are looking for mobile friendly websites. The days of most individuals using a desktop are gone. Your information should always be mobile friendly. Mobile friendly means it will work on a cell phone or a smartphone, tablets, watches, and the hybrids. It must automatically transfer from portrait to landscape view as I turn my device. Often people will change the view orientation to be able to see the information. Sometimes, when the direction is not addressed it may cause information or whole sections to disappear. Websites that are 3 to 5 years old, built before 2014, will have this issue if they are not updated.

You should have Google Analytics installed on your website. It's FREE! It will show you valuable information about how the public is viewing *Your Message*, for example how long they stay on your site; what they are looking at and for how long. See what they are searching for and even if they are a first time user or repeat viewer. It's truly valuable information for you as the business owner.

Your website will attract a lot more hits if you link it to your social media or other websites. Linking your site to others will make you more visible in Google search options. There should be links from your website to each type of social media you use. Also post links from your social media back to your website. The more cross clicks, the better. Also, consider finding a business that you have a symbiotic relationship with and crosslink their website to yours. The end results: the more links, the higher number of crosslinks, the more you will be elevated and appear in the search engines.

I thought for years that I was doomed to be the first person that would come up on the fourth page if you searched for "David Kauffman." There is a David Kauffman who is a musician, poet, and songwriter. He has always filled the first three pages with his many YouTube links. I thought "this is where I will always be, page 4". However, I recently checked as I was showing this to a client and discovered that I was half way up page 3!

How did this happen? Because I am a member of BNI Delaware Valley Regions I get my information posted on four websites. I then link my social media to those accounts. I now have enough crosslinks that I am moving up on the search pages. I am currently one of the first three listings on the top of page 3... page 2 here I come! However, people who pay will always appear at the top of the first page. The only way to surpass them is to pay more!

Do not use Flash Player on your website, since it may stop people with Apple devices from opening your links. If they find a broken link or a link they cannot open, they will leave your website without getting the information they were searching for. It will hurt *Your Message.*

How about slow loading pages? How long will people wait before they go elsewhere? This lag time may be the result of large pictures, lack of HTTP compression or several other reasons. How can this not affect *Your Message*? Data also shows if viewers leave due to this issue they won't be back! Consult with your web developer to maximize your load time.

Make sure you use a font that is easy to read on all devices; again if a potential client has any issue difficulty reading they are off to the next site.

Think about this scenario: You are on a website, and you are ready to sign on or hire the company. You pick up your phone and… you can't find any contact information. You click on this tab and that drop down box but still no phone number. You can't find it! You give up and are back to the search engine to find another site! Now unless you are one of those companies that really doesn't want to speak to their clients, like the airlines, this is a problem. Contacting your business should be easy. Your contact information should be on every footer of every page and easy to read. Adding your information on every page will ensure there is never an issue with anyone contacting you.

I am confident that if you own a website, you have been told about "keywords". It used to be that the more keywords you crammed into the text, the greater the chance you would be high on the search list. Now the spiders that search the web are so much smarter than in the past. Spiders are programs that search content on the web looking for certain words or phrases. They are also looking for how keywords are placed in the content, not just the amount of them on a page. So, make sure they are set correctly and in sets of threes in your content, meaning repeated three times on the page, but don't just pack them in. Again, have a professional help you, either a website developer or a company that specializes in search engine optimization. If you prefer to do it yourself there are many self-help websites.

Is the overall view of *Your Message* clear? I should be able to understand what you do and the object of your website within seconds of opening your home page. There should also be enough in the mix of style to have general appeal to all kinds of people looking for your services. Again, it should feel comforting and informative to all.

Now open your computer, your tablets and your cell phone, and look up your business website. How does *Your Message* look? Does it work on all three platforms? There are many types of people and they will often use more than one platform to view your website. Make sure your website works on ALL platforms.

There are many more questions to ask yourself but start with these. If the answers do not all appeal to your potential clients, if the links don't work, then it may be time to think about a makeover or a whole new website. It is always a good idea to have a professional look it over since it may be cost effective to start fresh. Don't do it alone, consult an expert.

You should also ask one of your clients to look it over and share his or her opinion. Ask people to test the functions and read the content. Does the site compel them to answer your call to action? Perhaps give them a few questions to answer by only looking at your website. Just remember there is no bad feedback. Don't get upset if they give you feedback that is not positive, or they view things differently.

Action Items

- ✓ Look at your website.
- ✓ Does it open easily? Can you read it on your phone?
- ✓ Does it switch from portrait to landscape when you turn your phone or tablet?

- ✓ Check all the links. Do they work and open quickly?
- ✓ Can I find your contact information on every page?
- ✓ Does it speak to the potential clients who are searching for your services or products?
- ✓ Do you have pictures that are yours?
- ✓ Is the content up to date?

CHAPTER 6
Social media, if you must

The average person spends between twenty minutes and six hours on social media every day (YouTube, Facebook, Twitter, Instagram and others). It's difficult to know what the correct number is, since there are so many studies and articles on the internet regarding this subject. The impact of social media leads to a difficult question for you and *Your Message*. Will your posts help or harm your image?

Postings on LinkedIn, Facebook, Twitter, Instagram, YouTube, and blogs are all forms of social media. They are also forms of networking. Networking is all about *Your Message*. Social media is one of the most efficient ways to get *Your Message* into the hands of the thousands of people who before the internet, cell phones, and tablets would never have known who you are or what type of business you have.

The problem with this method of communication is the potential to damage *Your Message* just as easily as to build it. Occasionally people can be alienated by businesses inundating them with information that doesn't feel relevant to them. If you are enlightening them with your viewpoints on social issues, religion, or politics and they see those issues differently, they may choose not to do business with you and your company. These types of posts should not be part of *Your Message*.

There is a theory I was taught years ago when I bought my travel agency franchise. The more people you can get in front of, the more clients you will have. It was called the three-foot rule. The premise was that everyone within three feet of you, at all times and locations, should have your business card and know what you do for a living. This type of thinking is old school and wrong. I hate to be the bearer of bad news to those of you still using this technique, but it doesn't work. Most people just don't care.

The few exceptions would be if those individuals need your service at that time, and that is rare, as a lawyer passing a slip and fall and reaching down to the person on the ground writhing in pain and handing him a card.

In 2002 my wife and I bought a house. It was what we in this area of Pennsylvania call a twin, meaning two homes sharing a common wall. After a few years, we decided to finish the third floor. It had a 15 foot high adjoining wall, and I decided I would use the third floor as a master bedroom suite. We left the common brick wall as it was, except we painted it. We hung our flat screen TV on it and put the bed on the opposite wall, the "low" side where the ceiling slanted. The chimney was in the far left front corner of the room on the shared wall, at the front of the house.

One night we were watching TV, and there was a bad nor'easter. It was pouring rain and very windy. After a while, the water began to run down the outside of the chimney. However, it never damaged the drywall ceiling, and it never got down to the floor. Now, in my position I work with over 3000 businesses, and know about 50 roofers, so who did I call? None of them, even though I had their contact information and knew most of them personally.

42

Why didn't I act? It just wasn't important. The water was not doing any damage to my house. It never reached the floor or damaged the ceiling. When did I finally call to have it fixed? When I went to sell the home, and I had to fill out the disclosure form given to me by the real estate agent that asked about water leaks. So, there goes the three-foot rule out the window!

Think about it another way, if you need to have your heart valve replaced, are you going to choose a surgeon because you were in a bar and he handed you his card, or would you be better selecting your surgeon from the yellow pages (ok, on the internet)? No, why not? It's because we want to know who we are doing business with and that they do it well. We want a personal recommendation, a close contact referral. Therefore, you will have a better chance with social media if you target *Your Message* to the correct group of people; those who need your services. Make sure you receive and post plenty of testimonials, and don't do mass postings since they have little or low value to the public.

Think about how many requests you receive to "like a page" from people you don't know or barely know. Don't you think if I liked it I would repost it or "like it" without you prompting me to do so? I do realize my thoughts go against what many marketing people will tell you, but you are not a megastore that can afford to lose a percentage of your clients because of excessive posting.

I surmise that whatever the total number of sincere "likes" on most social media business pages it's actually far less than what is posted. There are so many people who will "like" anything just to stop the requests for "liking" from coming.

People just love social media; the two I view most are Facebook and LinkedIn. Both can be used to help you get *Your Message* to the public and your target market. What you post represents your businesses. I wonder what people think as they post, or I guess I should say I wonder why people DON'T think before they post. It may weigh heavily, or at least make me concerned to do business with you, if your posts are far right or left. When I see posts that are political and maybe not my view, posts about anything that would cause me to pause before I use your business, you're in trouble. Hot topics like abortion and gun control should be avoided at all cost. Did you comment on sexual issues, gender, or woman's rights issues? If you post about issues like these, it will most likely not go well for you, as 50% of people will always disagree with you. These are posts for your private pages.

Let's look at how posting can cost you clients because of your opinions. What if I'm on the other side of an issue? What if I see the world differently than you? What if we are friends on Facebook or I follow your business and am offended by your thoughts? There are so many issues that people may see differently. For example, the killing of Cecil the lion, abortion, political views are all hotbeds of contention. Your comments on any of these could potentially cost you clients.

I am always stunned at what people post on their pages. There are people I once respected to whom I stopped sending clients after I read their posts on politics and social issues.

Now I am not telling you to change your opinions, just to think about your perspective target. If it is a public post, it's to the entire world. Maybe you just want to post to your personal contacts and not your entire client base? What about the person who feels it is so important that we all know his or her every move? I do not need to know how often you use the restroom or that you are at the gas station filling up, or that you just went to the food store, again. Choose your posts carefully, especially if you share personal and work posts at the same time. Too many posts may lead people to block you.

Look at your pictures, especially your profile picture. What message are you sending? Are you a party person? Do you have photos that show you frequently drinking or smoking something? What does your profile picture say about *Your Message*? Is it a good headshot with a bright business background, maybe some type of formal image, or is it a selfie on the beach or at a bar? Is there another person in the picture? Should he or she be in the picture? Was there someone in the picture, but now all you see is their arm around your shoulder, and the rest of the person is cut off? What do you think? Do you have a funky backdrop behind you, and you're on a slight tilt? Does it look like your child took the picture? Take a good look at your picture. What does it say about you? Then look at your friend's pictures and think about it. What does his or her message say? What does *Your Message* say?

Let's look at your posts. As I stated before, I think most of us do not realize that political posts cost us clients. I was watching the posts of a financial adviser I know well and thought very highly of, until now. He was posting extreme opinions about his political views, gun control, the issues of police shootings, and religion. The concern is they may and probably will offend some of his clients. It did offend me, and therefore I will not send him clients or hire him myself.

There are two options on how to fix or protect yourself from these issues. One is to keep your mouth shut in public! The second would be if you really need to voice your opinion, have two separate Facebook pages. Keep one clean and open to the public. On the second, private or personal page post all your crazy one sided politically charged posts; all your twisted and insane views on life and the world! Just make sure you only have non-business friends on this page, and hope they never repost your opinion on public pages. It is fine to post your opinions to your friends since they will most likely not affect your business.

Facebook, Instagram and LinkedIn may not be your friends! I have not covered the many other forms of social media, but they are also included in this discussion. When you visit Facebook and view other people's homepages or newsfeeds what do you see? Look at the pictures, posts, and comments. What do you think?

Ok, how about a self test?

Now look at your posts from the past year and review them. Look at them from the viewpoint of your clients. Most people don't think about the outcome or backlash from what they send out through social media. Do they think what the consequences might be when they post their opinions? Go back and take a good hard look. Are your posts about topics that would offend your clients or potential customers? You may think it was funny at the time, or you were angry at something going on in the world, but would your clients feel the same way? Did you post about topics that are polarizing? Delete those posts and refrain from these types of posts on the business side of your social media.

It is never too late to change; people tend to remember what you did last, not what you did best, so post a positive message today.

Action Items

- ✓ Look at your Social Media, LinkedIn, Facebook, Instagram. What do you see?
- ✓ Will your posts offend someone?
- ✓ Do your pictures look unprofessional?

CHAPTER 7
Blogging: Should I, could I, would I

Just like the other aspects of *Your Message* we have examined, blogging will have an impact on your business. But how can blogging effect *Your Message*? The answer is definitely in your hands. *Your Message* can be positive or negative. Where should you blog, Facebook, LinkedIn, your website, or a repetitive email to your clients? What you blog about, how often and the quality of the content all affect *Your Message*.

Blogging can be an excellent way to establish yourself as an expert in your field or create a following. But blogging, too, can damage *Your Message*. If you include information that is political or offensive, it will cost you clients. But this is not the only issue with blogging. A lack of consistent information can convince me not to do business with you. Blogs can also lead to trouble when you are posting personal issues in your life. Do we need to have all that information? If you are having a problem with a client then you post about it, then the client reads your blog, now what? If you talk about your personal issues, do people care? Will they stop returning to your site?

A friend of mine thought he would enhance his brand by starting a blog. Sounds good, I thought; he would blog about his home maintenance business. Again, this is a topic many people would follow. He decided to use Facebook as his platform. Then he posted his first blog. I should have told you he has a handyman service company with one employee. His first set of topics was about winter proofing a house before the cold weather set in. He had music playing in the background. In my opinion it was bad music, some type of electronic crap. He included a checklist, all good, but he only gave a partial list! He cut it off and told his audience there was a fee for the complete list.

The second post was a week later. He blogged about looking for locations in your house that might need more insulation to reduce energy costs in the upcoming winter months. Ok, a good topic, but still with the bad music. Post three, now three weeks after the last post: ceiling fans and the winter months. Again, a good follow up topic. Sadly, again still the bad music blasting in the background. Five weeks after the last post came another post: what to do with your outdoor central air conditioning unit and then, silence, nothing. Two months passed, and no post. Then out of the blue, a post. Four months had passed, and he decided to blast out a message about spring cleaning.

I called and asked, "Why the post? I assumed you had given up." He told me a client who had used his company for many years thought he had gone out of business when the posts stopped, so he had to start again.

What went wrong? Where to begin, since so much of his attempts to be a blogger failed? Ok, there was some content, but that was about it. There was no long term plan. A few things he should have thought of; the blog should not have tried to sell content, he should have skipped the music, his blogging schedule was inconsistent and then it stopped.

The platform is critical; you need to know your audience or your targeted audience. Was Facebook the right platform for his business? How many "friends" did he have, and were they personal or business friends? Would they see the value of his blogs and tell others to follow him? Was it a business, a personal, or a combination of the two? Again, who are you speaking to? Who do you want to talk to? Is it your current clients and friends or are you using the posts to drive business to your company?

So, let's look at the good and bad of blogging, remembering it directly reflects *Your Message*. People might not care for your taste in music. Bad music, or any music, can make people move on in seconds to a different page. Just don't do it; keep your music on your personal devices.

How easy is your blog to read? If I struggle to read it, I am gone. Dark blue background and white text? Oh no. Crazy fonts? I'm gone. A little color in the background is ok but keep it light, with black or very dark color text.

We have short attention spans. The title and the first line are essential to get me to stay and continue to read your blog. If I have to scroll up and down on your site page to find excellent content on a particular topic, then "click," I'm gone and off to the next web page. You must catch my attention in the first few lines.

Be careful not to get lazy and start copying another person's stuff. Plagiarism is never acceptable. It's illegal. And you certainly don't want to get caught using someone else's information and claiming it is yours. It is so easy to check if you are using someone else's information. I have a program that will search over eight billion web pages to check for plagiarism. You need to get permission and make sure you credit the person or website for their content.

You need to have quality content that makes me want to bookmark your page. Content is very important if you are trying to drive business to your company. It's all right to post small blogs to stretch them out. But every blog should provide value to your audience. Content, pictures, ideas, even color and font schemes can all have an impact on *Your Message.*

Don't try to be an expert if you're not! You need to find a niche you are passionate about or a topic that is part of your profession. The handyman blogging about winter checklists for your house was well within his expertise. Remember, your blog should add value to *Your Message.*

Don't be a bore. You must be interesting. Add some humor. If your blog is too technical, with no stories or anecdotes, your audience will find it difficult to read, and they may not return.

Many of my clients have tried to get me to blog; the answer is NO. Why? I know at some point I will not feel like writing on a strict schedule. I enjoy writing on my time. I was at a meeting with new clients, who had decided to blog. "Ok," I asked, "how often?" Their response was twice a week. I looked at them and said, "Great that means 104 blogs per year!" I enjoyed the look on both of their faces! One of them looked at me and replied, "I never thought of it like that." There was a bit of silence and then they agreed to cut it back to once a week. For weeks after, each time we met, one of them said the most valuable piece of information that came out of our first meeting was the eye opening statement, "That's 104 blogs per year!"

If you blog and gain a following, you cannot stop, or it will be very difficult to stop! If you do stop and don't tell your readers you're ending the series, *Your Message* will be affected. One of two things will happen. First, when they log on and there is no new post, you will lose your credibility. Second, even worse, they may think you went out of business. You can blog in short spurts if your audience knows this will be a short series of blogs about a specific topic and it will end in "blank" weeks. Make sure you let them know when the next series will start. So, write ahead. If you are going to blog, be sure to write twelve blogs before your first post. Every time you post make sure you replace it, so you will always have twelve as a backup. If you do this, it will ensure that you have plenty of content to post, even if you don't feel like writing for a few weeks.

The next question that comes up is when to post. That is a difficult question. It depends on what you are blogging about and the platform or number of platforms you are using, the topic of your blog, and last but most important, how you will accomplish this. Once you start releasing your blog, you need to continue to do so at regular intervals, once a day, week, or month. It is all about a consistent message being sent.

Should you have a picture of yourself on your blog? It's probably a good idea to do so. People want to see who is speaking to them. But just as on your business card and social media, make it a good, current, professional one.

So, if you are going to venture into the world of blogging, think it through. There is no hurry to get started. Look at other blogs that have been going for a while and see how others are using this platform. What do you like or dislike about what you see? Set a goal for your blog and stick to the strategy. Plan it out and remember, it is going to be an ongoing part of *Your Message.*

Action Items

- ✓ Look at the number of blogs you want to post.
- ✓ Write ahead, at least 12.
- ✓ Look at the written text; is it easy and clear to read?

CHAPTER 8

Email: Yes, they matter and so do texts

Many people write and reply to emails without realizing emails are a huge part of their message. How you write and respond to emails has a significant impact on how people view you and your business. Always remember your emails are representing *Your Message*. Spelling, format, grammar, word choice, and capitalization are all parts of how we view you. The worst issue is when you do not respond at all. How do your clients even know if you ever received their email if there is no reply or a long delay in your response?

I receive a lot of emails every day. I average well over 100 new emails each and every day. You would not believe what I read. The best, or shall I say the worst, of them has a message but nothing else. No name, business name, or any contact information; just a message. "I am looking for information on your new chapter. Thanks." How do you reply to this? You look at the email address for some hope of a clue, but scaryboy178@gmail.com is not very revealing. What type of message does an email address like scaryboy178@gmail.com say to your customers? Other emails are written so poorly I am amazed. No punctuation, poor grammar, spelling errors, no idea of proper capitalization. Do they not have spell check on their computers? Now I know sometimes we miss an error, but that is not what I am referring too.

Once in a while we all send out an email we wish we had looked at a bit closer before sending. There was one I sent out to a client; it was funny, but pretty embarrassing!

Sent from Client:

On Nov 23, 2016, at 10:11 AM, XXXXXX XXXXX

Need to cancel our meeting tomorrow.

On Nov 23, 2016, at 12:09 PM, David Kauffman <davidk@YourBusinessBasics.com> wrote:

Got tit, thanks! Enjoy the holiday.

Response from the client:

Didn't use spell check uh? Yes, I have 2 of them. Lol!! Happy Thanksgiving to you as well!

Sent from my iPhone XXX XXX XXXX

So even when you are careful, sometimes things get overlooked. Don't rely on spell check for the right words. You need to read what you wrote. These are some examples of words that spell check can miss:

one – won

too – two – to

then – than

there – their

maid – made

sail – sale

You need to be your own grammar and spell check.

Your perception can also create an issue. When you write things, you perceive in your mind what you wanted to say. You can read and read, and still, your mind sees what it wants to.

Many years ago, when I was working on my travel agency. I created my new business card with a friend of mine. We went back and forth over what should be on it. We got down to the end, and I sent it to the printer. He sent me the final proof and told me to read it, read it again out loud, read it to my wife, and I did. It was sent to the printer, and a few days later I received the box at my office. I was so happy. "Yay," new business, new cards! I was ready to go! I opened it and looked them over. I was so happy until I got to my 800 number. The last four numbers were transposed. I called my friend and he started to laugh! Shall I reorder them?

What about those who type in all capitals? I thought it was just someone who had no idea about capitalization, so he or she just kept it all in capitals. No, I found out from one of my daughters as she was looking over my shoulder, and asked, "Why is she so mad?" I had no idea this was someone yelling at me. Who knew?

Emails have no emotion, or do they? How can you tell the tone of the message when there is no inflection of voice? Worse is if I construe information in the email that is something that was not the intention of the author.

Poor punctuation can also be a problem. It can show a lack of knowledge or a lack of understanding. It can also change the meaning of the sentence altogether.

What is the simplest correct way to punctuate this sentence?

A woman without her man is nothing

A woman without her man is nothing.

A simple period is a correct answer. You may not all like the meaning, but it is correct. Let's try again.

A woman, without her man, is nothing.

Ok, this is also a correct answer, and again you may not all like the meaning, but it is correct. Let's try again.

A woman: without her, man is nothing.

The same sentence, with a third meaning. I would assume most of the female readers are much happier with this version. Yes, the grammar is correct on all three examples, but the meaning is entirely different.

Another example:

Let's eat grandpa! or Let's eat, grandpa!

Same sentence different meaning, especially to grandpa.

We're going to learn to cut and paste kids!
   or
We're going to learn to cut and paste, kids!

I do believe the parents would prefer the second sentence.

Example from someone's resume: Interests include: Cooking dogs, shopping, dancing, reading, watching movies …

Maybe a comma after cooking would have been in order.

How about these:

I think they should remove the period after someone to correct the meaning of their sign.

I love this example.

Rachael Ray finds inspiration in cooking her family and her dog,
   or
Rachael Ray finds inspiration in cooking, her family, and her dog.

I think her family and her dog would feel much better if they had added a few commas.

These were examples from Cyber text news letter https://cybertext.wordpress.com/2012/11/22/a-light-hearted-look-at-how-punctuation-can-change-meaning/

Greetings should also be considered. If you see someone in a store or call on the phone would you jump right into a question or statement? No, we always start off with a greeting: Hello, how are you, or something to that effect. But too often an email has no greeting. What message is that communicating to the person who received it? Cold and uncaring.

How about your email address? What is it and where is it hosted? Years ago, I didn't think much of this, but as I spoke to people about it and asked their opinions, I began to realize it is very important. Does it end in AOL? This does say you have been in business a long time, but it also means you have not changed with the times and might be outdated. Many business people use free providers like Gmail or Yahoo. Gmail is my personal favorite. I have six email addresses, and I use Gmail as a platform or a mail collector. It makes my life easier to go to one location.

If you are looking at this from your client's eyes, however, it may say something entirely different. You could look at David_Yourbusinessbasics@gmail.com and think cheap and unprofessional. This issue is also true for emails that end in Comcast.net, Verizion.com, Yahoo, AOL, or Gmail.com. Some of these companies, like Gmail will give you the ability to change it to your business name for a small fee.

Which looks better as part of *Your Message*?

David_yourbusinessbasics@gmail.com

   or

David@YourBusinessBasic.com

If your email address ends in the name of your business *Your Message* will reflect professionalism and there will be no question about who you are.

I may be getting old but why is it we no longer have the time to spell out a word? Emails are not a text and texts still need to be understood! I am speaking about business text more than personal. I find it hard to understand all of the abbreviations. Dk (don't know), tx u (text you). Really can't type one more letter? w/w (wall to wall), smh (shaking my head), dn (did not), lmk (let me know), or @ (at). I am sure there are so many others I haven't been exposed to. Then we skip the letters altogether and just use emojis. It seems as if we are heading back to the time of hieroglyphics. What message are you sending? IML... I AM LAZY.

When sending a text remember you may not be in their contact list. I receive messages from people asking questions or for information assuming I know who they are. I often have to send back the question "Who is this?". So always include your name unless you are sure you're in their contact list.

Last on my list of how to destroy *Your Message* through email is SPAM. I know there are so many types of software to track and keep you in contact with your clients. Stop and think. It's not about you, right? So, do they want your emails? Did they ask to receive them? Even worse is when you send these types of emails, and there is no way to unsubscribe or opt out. There are laws in the United States and

Canada that are very strict about this type of email. So besides making the recipients angry at your company or you, it may violate the law.

Think, think, think! Oh, yes, and think some more! What are you saying, how are you saying it? How does *Your Message* look to those who receive your emails? Tone and inflection are all lost in an email. What did you mean? How can I tell? So many times, I have read an email and wondered, what the message is. There have been many times over the years when I sent emails to clients, and they were received the wrong way. I have gone back and read them, and seen why. I was not clear in my message. These were the times it was brought to my attention; I am sure there were others when it was not. How many times did I do this and maybe lose a client, or made the client think twice about using my company? I may never know. Do you?

How do we prevent these mistakes from affecting our relationships with our clients? I would always recommend you write your emails in Word or another word processing program. Using this format will allow you to make sure the spelling and punctuation are correct. Read it a few times to make sure it makes sense. Read it from the recipient's eyes. Can *Your Message* be taken in more than one way? Remember, there is no tone of voice or inflection in words in email. Things can be taken the wrong way, so you need to be very clear. Never respond out of anger. It is not the message you want to put out to the public.

Think for a minute. How long does an email last? Forever and ever! Once you hit the send button, it is now in the hands of another who can forward it, save it, or post it for all to see! If it is not an email you would be proud to read to the recipient in front of witnesses, maybe you should change the content or decide not to send it at all.

Action Items

- ✓ Think before you send.
- ✓ Don't be lazy — write words out.

CHAPTER 9
Basic communication, or lack thereof

Getting clients or potential clients to understand *Your Message* is a genuinely challenging problem. Every time you meet someone, it becomes a networking event. The obvious meetings are at the many types of networking events. The most common are the chambers of commerce events and business card exchanges, but what about other business meetings, chance encounters in food or other stores, parking lot run ins? These are all networking events, and your speech matters!

The principal issue is we just don't think about how we sound to others. We rarely even care if they understand what we are trying to communicate. We speak to ourselves. We tend to blurt out information they don't need or want. The recipient of this information might not even care about *Your Message*. We speak to ourselves with little thought of our clients' views or understanding.

I have attended hundreds of networking events, conferences, and presentations. Over time, I have listened to thousands of business owners attempt to communicate a productive weekly presentation, also known as an elevator speech, and they usually fail miserably. Why? Most often it's because they are speaking to themselves or about themselves. I would say almost always it's because they have no idea how to get their message out clearly, or what the correct message is for their audience. They talk as if we all understand what they are thinking and know the terms of their business. They use terms or acronyms specific to their industry. Again, to whom is the message being delivered? I think by now you know the answer!

When you think about it, you need many different messages, because you will speak to an array of potential clients or people who can send you new customers. Most of us have many products and services to offer. First, think about where you are and to whom you are speaking. *Your Message* needs to be different depending on where you are, how long you will have to talk, and what you are trying to achieve.

In almost every case, less is more, so much more. You want people to ask you questions, ask for a second meeting, or offer you one of their contacts. Think about where you are going and then make sure you have thought out a productive message. Remember you represent *Your Message* no matter where you are.

Every message at a formal networking event should have a call to action or an attention getter. It may be:

A good referral for me is……,

Did you know that…, Have you ever seen…,

Have you heard someone complaining about…?

I would like to meet or have an introduction to …

This type of statement will give recipients a reason to listen vs. you rambling on about your business.

Stay away from generic words: anyone, anybody, any business. Be very specific as to what you want or need. You never know who I know. When *Your Message* is generic, their response will also be generic… most likely not what you are seeking.

Only one topic per message, we love to spill our guts to all who will listen. Do they need all that information; do they care? You need to consider where you are in the relationship. Is this the first or second meeting? Are they asking for more information? Is the person you are speaking to ready for further communication? Is the relationship ready to go to the next level?

Clarify the size of the business you are looking to work with, small, medium, large. How many employees does it have? If you ask ten people the question, "How many employees does a large company have?" You will get ten different answers. What is the type of business, the name, and who, specifically is the person you want to meet?

Do not talk about your products unless you are answering a question that was directly asked of you. For the most part people will have an idea what you do by the name of the business. Remember, people need to want to do business with you before they engage in the process. If you sell your products or services to them on your first meeting, it may not go well. The exception to this is if you are the showcase at an event, or you are a paid sponsor. These events usually have booths or are chamber mixers. They will be product based events and maybe have booths or tables like trade shows. Even at these events, *Your Message* should be about meeting new people and not attempting to close the deal.

If you are in a group of individuals, it is best to have a standalone message. When speaking about *Your Message*, it should not be confused with others. Do not share a topic or "piggyback" off another person in the group when speaking.

If you want to be introduced to a particular person, you may need to meet someone else first. I was at a networking event in Villanova, PA when someone asked to be introduced to the head of the facilities department of Bryn Mawr College. I don't know who he or she is. However, I do know the head of the IT department, so I ask the member if that introduction would be valuable to him? His response was yes since he was sure that person would be working with the facilities department. I may not know the owner of the company, but I may know an employee. Start with, "I am trying to meet the owner of 'X' company, but I would be happy to meet someone at the business who can make the right connection."

The truth is you may need to ask for help to find out how *Your Message* is being received by others. Just understand you may not like what you hear. Contact your existing clients and ask them a few questions. How did I do when we spoke last? Do I communicate well? If you are at a networking event, again ask someone if he or she understood *Your Message* and what you were asking?

When you are going to a networking event, set a goal. Why are you going? What do you want to leave with? Who will you be speaking to? Now go back and read this chapter again and craft a message that will bring you the desired results. Always prepare ahead of time. You should master some short presentations that you can deliver on a moment's notice. Remember, think before you speak.

Action items

- ✓ Call your own numbers and listen to how you sound.
- ✓ Write out a few short presentations about your business and practice and memorize them, so they will come naturally when needed.

CHAPTER 10
Why do I need to speak to you

Why do I need to speak to you? We have all this technology surrounding us! Did you ever stop to think that people will want to talk to you the owner, the expert? Sometimes the importance of person to person communication is viewed as old school, but I disagree. Communication, and the style of it, are too frequently overlooked by businesses. Both owners and sales people alike miss the importance of this concept. Young professionals often overlook communication problems without even realizing it is an issue.

There is a company I worked with, and I thought I would send them a friend of mine who needed their services. I sent a referral with the contact information, expecting the owner to call and set up an appointment for an estimate. But this is what happened; some office assistant called my friend and wanted to set up the meeting. "Who are you?", she asked. "Why is Tom not calling me? I was expecting him to call; that's what David told me".

Thanks, but no thanks. What happened to the personal touch? It seems it has been lost with some other essential business etiquette. This type of communication may be business lost, because a decision was made that the office staff should be the first contact instead of the person who was referred. What are you telling your referrals with that action? I am too busy to take the time to make calls. If a referral comes from an existing client or from a referral group, you need to be first contact. After that, if the client is ok with a call from your office staff for future communication, that's totally acceptable.

A second example of a referral that went bad is as follows; I referred a client to a contractor. The office assistant called back and told my client he lived too far away, and he should find a contractor closer to his home, and it would cost him less money. Now I know the owner would have traveled a bit out of his geographic area for a quality referral. It was a referral from me and I was an existing client. Never let an office assistant take your place and make business decisions better left to the owner. These types of issues may cost you a single client or even a stream of referrals from that client.

Another form of communication disconnect that is fairly new in the business world is an electronic assistant. A business associate was telling me about this great new way to manage his time. It is a type of artificial intelligence. I know, how cool right? But what does this say about *Your Message*? You, the client, are not worth the owner's time. I don't need to speak to you. This is even worse than the first story of the office assistant who calls in your place. Now it is a digital voice replacing you or more disturbing is masked as an email system to set appointments. I was working with a young startup company and the owner had set up his email so that anytime he received a new contact the owner would push a button and this computer program would take over. "Hi, I am Mary's office assistant. I would like to set an appointment for you to …," This email was not an authentic communication from the owner. It was a computer, not a person. The owner should be calling or sending a personal email as the first contact.

I was at networking event speaking to a friend about this issue. When a younger business person who was a life insurance agent standing with us joined into the conversation. He brought up the topic of artificial intelligence being the first contact vs a real person. He thought there was nothing wrong with having a computer act as the first contact. I spoke of the disconnect it can cause and how this could affect your business and he was amazed by my opinion. He told me he always had office staff call to set up the appointments with his clients, and that he never thought about how it would feel from the viewpoint of potential customers. I told them a story about a networking expert who had wanted to meet me because she felt we would work well together. A sales trainer I knew had told her about me and my work. However, she had her personal assistant call me to set up an appointment which I felt was very impersonal and somewhat demeaning, especially since she expressed interest initially about meeting me. I told her personal assistant I wanted to speak directly with her before setting up a meeting. I didn't want to meet with her if she couldn't take the time to pick up the phone and call me directly. I never received the call. Her loss.

The topic of artificial intelligence and computer driven personal assistants is becoming a growing issue in the business world. I understand the convenience of having such a system. Be careful of trying to appeal to one type of client at the expense of all others. *Your Message* needs to attract a wide variety of people all having different needs. Younger people are excited about the new programs and how they save them time in setting up appointments, and the more seasoned generation may prefer to use a personal assistant or office manager to make the first call, but the issue is the same. People want a personal touch.

Another area to consider is that we tend not to think about the voicemails we leave on clients' phones. Have you ever received a message without a name or return number? "Hey, I need to speak to you about an issue I am having with your company, please call me back, thanks." Have you done this? Have you received these messages?

When you leave a voicemail message for someone, think about what he or she will hear when it's played back. Speak clearly, leave your full name and number, the reason for your call, and the best time to reach you. You also want to let him or her know if you need an urgent response.

How can you repair this problem? Well, there's a simple solution: pick up of the phone! It's never an issue if the appointment or the estimate is set up by your office or personal assistant or even by a computer, but only *after* I speak to the business owner I was referred to. "Hello, my name is David from Your Business Basics, I received your information from Tom. Would it be all right if I have Mary, my assistant, call you to set up a time for us to meet? She is my life saver; she keeps me on track by setting all my appointments." It's that simple.

If you want to use the newer type of office assistant, like the AI programs, just ask. "Hi, my name is David. I received your request for an estimate, would it be ok with you if I brought in my computerized assistant? She sets all my meetings and helps me manage my time. This allows me to be as efficient as I can be with my time." Then it's a yes or no, but at least you won't lose a client because you offended him or her with your lack of personal attention.

Action items

- ✓ Review your process.
- ✓ Set aside the time to make the first call.

CHAPTER 11

Follow up, follow up, follow up, or the absence thereof

The slow death, or sometimes a bit quicker, of any business is ignoring its clients. What does that mean to you? Have you called a company and left a message on their voicemail or with an answering service, or maybe spoke to a gatekeeper? Then you wait to hear back from them. One day, two, three days go by. But the return call never comes. You wait for a few more days or maybe even longer, and no response. You call back and leave another message, and still no one contacts you? What is their message to you? It would appear that they do not want or need your business.

Did you ever contact a contractor who came to your house or business; spoke a good game about his or her service and how he or she will do a great job? He or she looked at the work to be done, told you that you would hear back shortly, and you never received the estimate or proposal? Did you call back to ask for it and still they make you wait weeks to get it, or it never arrives?

Have you been in a situation where you were given an estimate, you agree to the price and terms, and even then, contractors disappear. No calls, no contact, just gone! When someone asks you for a recommendation, what will you say? People are much more talkative about a negative experience than a positive one. You will hear the entire story of how they were ignored no matter what you did.

For many years, I have been in BNI, a closed contact network group. It helped me grow all my businesses, from the electrical contracting company to my travel agency that were started with no clients and grew to over 300 clients, all by word of mouth referrals. I am telling you this because this won't happen without regular and consistent follow up on any type of referral, big or small. Follow up is crucial, but when the referral comes from a friend or business associate it takes it to another level of importance.

There was a contractor in my group, who would received many referrals every month. He would take them and look them over. Next, he would think about how busy he was at the time. Most often he had enough work booked to pay his bills. So, those referral slips would end up in the glove compartment of his truck. A month or two later when the work was slow, and there was not enough cash to pay the bills, out they would come. By then, however, it was too late. The potential clients had moved on, and the relationship with the person who gave him the referral destroyed. How many future referrals were lost as a result of this oversight!?

Remember, if you do a great job people will tell others. Great work and follow up will result in spin-off business.

Let's say you were asked for a good painter by a client you considered a friend. You tell him about your painter. You give your client the contact information and assume it will all go well. As expected, you get feedback from your client that the painter did a great job, so you know there was business completed and money paid. You expect a call or email from the painter, but no, there is not so much as a thank you from the painter you recommended. Will you send him another prospect?

Over the years, as discussed previously, I owned and operated several businesses, including an electrical contracting business, an alarm company, a travel agency, and a general contracting firm. They all relied heavily on referrals, as do most businesses. I was always amazed at how many times I went out on estimates and listened to the stories of failed communication with potential clients by other contractors.

All they had to do was to maintain a line of dialogue, show up on time for the estimate and get it back to the client in a reasonable time frame. This seems to be so easy and clear cut! These were clients that were prepared to pay out large sums of money, well not all of them, but most of them, to complete these high end jobs, but received no response from the contractor. *Business and spin-off business lost! Your Message* now has the perception of "I don't care, and don't use me or recommend me." I just never understood this behavior.

What are some of the many parts of follow up?

- ✓ Reply to a phone message promptly, best practice would be in less than 24 hours.
- ✓ Call a referral you receive within 24 hours.
- ✓ Respond to your clients after the initial contact, before they call you for information. Get the proposal back to them quickly. If things are going slowly or you are backed up and drowning in paperwork, just call and let them know you are thinking of them and their project.
- ✓ If you don't hear back from the client after you gave the proposal call to find out why.

- ✓ Thank the client who sent you a new prospect, just to let him or her know you care and appreciate the referral. Thanking your referral source is key to developing a steady stream of referrals.
- ✓ The thank you can be either by phone, email, letter or card.

Poor follow up is often just a lack of organization. But to your clients, it just means you don't care. If you don't keep track of what you need to do, how can other things not slip through the cracks? There are many types of software out there that can help you track your clients and the step by step process of communication. There are also some simple solutions. Writing everything in a spiral notebook is the most basic of all systems. When you have completed the event or task, cross it off. Another way is to use a digital calendar like Google or Outlook and put all your tasks into the calendar. Next, set up reminders on the calendar and you're on your way to great communication. Look at it each day or have your calendar send you a reminder when a task needs to be completed, and then do it.

The reality is communication is a crucial part of *Your Message*. It can set the tone for a long, profitable relationship or end it quickly. Go back and look at the list of new clients you have obtained over the past year, or even those clients who have used you again and again and contact them. Let them know you are thinking of them. If they are new clients, thank them by phone and find out how they found your business. If it was a referral from existing clients, call and thank them too. You should follow up on all contacts even if they are not a good fit for your business. Refer them to another company that would be better able to help them. It will make *Your Message* a positive one to all who have contact with you, and they will tell others of your kindness.

Now figure out a way to track your clients going forward and let them know you appreciate their business. Select a software program to help you or create your own. Start today. Use a simple notebook, so no one falls through the cracks. Excel will also work if you set up a spread sheet with dates and times. *Your Message* should be a grateful one. Always let clients know you appreciate them.

When it comes to the second contact, or follow up after the work is completed, you can use the same system to track all open jobs or tasks. Again, any of the methods I described will work. When you receive the first call or contact, put it into the system and follow up as needed. If you are going to a client's business or house for an estimate, give a time frame for the formal estimate to be delivered, and make sure it gets out on time! Never make the client call or reach out to you for the follow up.

Action Items

- ✓ Do you keep track of the time between contact?
- ✓ Look over the last few months, did someone slip through the cracks?
- ✓ Look into a simple system to make sure things such as return calls do not fall into the cracks.

CHAPTER 12

How do you look, or should I say how should you look

When I ask how you look, I am not asking if you could be on the cover of a fashion magazine, but about your basic appearance to others. Your presentation, clothing, cleanliness, even your hair is one of the first parts of *Your Message*, and people will judge you. When you are in a face to face meeting within the first few seconds people will form opinions about you.

If you want *Your Message* to be heard, you need to dress the part. When you see people at a networking event, business meeting, or even at a local restaurant during a business lunch, don't you judge them? Have you ever found that after your first view of some of them, you ask yourself, "Do they own a mirror?" "Did they put any thought into how they look to others?" My grandmother used to say" They should see themselves through my eyes."

Think about how often, you meet someone new, you look him or her over from head to toe and form your opinion. Have you been to an event and maybe you are speaking to a friend or associate and look across the room, and there's the vision? Your first thoughts, what was he or she thinking, how can anyone leave the house in that outfit? Next, you point the outfit out to your friend and you both have a laugh.

At a recent networking event a financial advisor came up to introduce himself. He shook my hand, and I looked at him only to see he was wearing a button down shirt not tucked in (that's ok, not great, but ok), shorts (not really ok), and open toed sandals (that's definitely not ok). I look down and see he has really hairy feet. All that comes to mind are the insurance commercials with the Neanderthal Man! Would I even be able to hear his message, let alone the fact that he's a financial advisor who wants me to hand over my life savings, when he's dressed like he's going to the beach?

How could I recommend him and his disgustingly hairy feet to my friends, my family, or any of my clients? How would he appear at my mother's home? Would I ever hear the end of it after that? I can hear it now; "So, your friend came to see me. I had to look at his toes, and they had lots of hair on them." What does that mean to others? "Was he on his way to the beach and just stopped by? What type of person did you send to my house? How can I trust him with my retirement accounts?"

What about my best clients? How would they view my decision to recommend him, shorts and sandals, and hairy toes? Every time I see this type of outfit all can think is, I would never, could never, refer him and his bare feet. Believe it or not, we will judge you by your appearance. Therefore, your presentation becomes a tool of *Your Message*. I am not speaking of whether you are thin or stout, but basic hygiene and appearance. I am talking about well kept hair; long or short it needs to be well kept.

There was a photographer who was in one of my chapters. He would roll into the meeting at the last minute. His hair was a mess, and clothes disheveled. He appeared to have skipped shaving for a few days. What did this mean to members he is looking to get business referrals from? One day I pulled him aside and asked what he was thinking? His response, I am developing the artistic look and feel for my business. Not really, because in fact when you asked the others in the room, he was designing the look of a non-referable business person.

How many of you think about your breath or your hands? A wet handshake can set the tone for a poor message. How do you smell, not just your breath? Smell, in general, can be a very touchy issue. It is hard to tell someone they stink like my 16 year old's shoes at the end of the summer (he never wore socks). Bad breath is also tough to deal with. Do you offer a mint? It even gets worse if he or she is a close talker!

Is your overall appearance appropriate in a professional business setting?

Now, if you are a tradesman how does this effect *Your Message*? Shorts in the summer, I get it. It's hot outside, but how are others looking at you? Having owned several contracting businesses, I think I have a good idea about this perspective. Shorts are acceptable. They are appropriate, but cutoff jeans are not.

I had a contractor come to my house in August. It was hot, so shorts would be appropriate. However, they were blue camouflage. Not professional. His shirt was a dirty red tee shirt, no business logo or name. I told him he needed to wear solid color shorts and shirts with his company name on them. He was shocked. He never thought it mattered. It is all right to wear jeans if you are a contractor, if they are clean. A three button shirt with a collar or tee shirt is fine, again if it is business professional and clean, and has your company name on it.

I was at a networking event with the local chamber and was introduced to a contractor. He may be great at what he does, but his shirt had another company's logo and name on it. What does that say? Unprofessional and CHEAP and advertising for another company!

You need to keep in mind, and I will come back to this over and over again: to whom are you speaking? What are you saying? Remember it is not about you. I am the customer. I am the judge and jury. I will decide if you and your business is the right match for my clients and me.

Where is the event? What type of event is it? Start with that and then stop and think. If you are heading to your office and there is no chance a client will see you, how should you dress? If you are going to the post office and you bump into a client, what will she think? If there will be a client stopping in on a whim with no notice, it becomes a business meeting, what will they think when they see you?

This thought process also has a lot to do with what your profession is and what the setting of your encounter might be. Most of the time business casual will do just fine.

Now, if you are going to a networking event you need to dress for *Your Message*. I can tell you that it is always great to be the best dressed person in the room. You feel good, and it presents the right message to those around you when you stand out. I have been to many events only to wish I was better dressed. Two ways to think about this: dress as if you are going to an interview for the most important job of your life, or as Dr. Ivan Misner once said to me, "Always dress at, or a step above, the level of your target audience. Don't dress below.

The better you look, the better *Your Message*. Remember you only get one chance to create a first impression and once it is formed, it will be nearly impossible to change.

How can you make sure *Your Message* is correctly received? This one is simple. You need to look in the mirror before you leave your house! Make sure you see yourself from the perspective of the person you will be meeting. I wish some of the people at the Jersey shore practiced this, or maybe not, as it does give us conversation all day as they parade down the beach. You need to look as if you are going to interview for an important job every time you have a business meeting! Don't be the one with the hairy feet; it just won't end well, I promise!

Action items

- ✓ Get in the habit of thinking about your appearance before you leave your house.
- ✓ Think about where you are going, and make sure you're dressed for the occasion.
- ✓ What will others think about how you look?!

CHAPTER 13

Outside events, formal and informal

We have discussed your appearance, and this is especially important when attending outside events. Outside events for our purpose will refer to formal or informal networking events. This idea of appearance will also come into play every time you are out in public. However, there is a bit of a free pass when you are just out and about running errands, since you are not technically representing *Your Message*. There may be many potential clients around you, no matter where you are. An outside event could also be at the gym or local hardware store, anywhere you run into an existing client or a potential new client. So, *Your Message* is out there for all to see all the time.

There are many mistakes people who go to formal networking events make. These can destroy, or at least damage, *Your Message*. When you are at a networking event, all aspects of *Your Message* that we have looked at are on public display. How do you look? When you speak, how do you sound? What materials are you handing out? All these things are significant. You have heard it before: you only get one chance to create a great first impression, and it is almost impossible to change it.

Understanding who you are communicating with at these events and respecting his or her style and the purpose for attendance is critical.

Why is he or she at the event? What does he or she want or need to get from the event?

Just in case you're unsure, it is essential to pay for your meal or entrance fee every time you attend a networking event. If not, others may view you and our businesses in a bad light. They may see you as cheap, or think you are tight with money, or worse yet, that your company has no money.

Never allow people to hear you complain about the fees. Again, you may seem cheap and unprofessional, even if you think they are your friends. Do you really know what they are thinking? It will become a direct reflection of you and *Your Message*. It's always about networking, not the fee, and it doesn't matter if you will eat or not. Serious networkers are never worried about costs or paying for a meal; they know why they are at the event and have a clear goal. So, pay for yourself since it doesn't matter if you eat, drink or only network. It is part of *Your Message* — make it a good one.

Asking for referral fees should never be on your mind. Those who give of themselves will get far more in return than a small referral fee. I understand there are certain professions in which fees are built into the culture, but that should be the byproduct, not the goal.

There are a few great books written on this topic. The best I have read is *The Go-Giver,* written by Bob Burg and John David Mann. Networkers who ask for referral fees genuinely do not understand how networking works. The most exceptional networkers realize that giving is what is essential. BNI got it right from the start. Their philosophy is "Givers Gain`, what goes around comes around!" If you give of yourself, it will come back to you tenfold.

How about the **card takers**? Give me your business card and I will give you mine. Why? The respected networkers understand there are those who only want to build their database through this collection process. You should think about whether the person is someone you feel would fit in with your networking or business goals. If so, then you can exchange cards, but also think about what the other's goals are or may be. Don't jump in and spread your cards too fast. It may be that you need to give of yourself and help, even though there will be no return in sight, to achieve your goals.

Some business people think that giving you their card is an automatic "yes" to have a business meeting, maybe over coffee, or even that you will sign on the dotted line. Why? What is the purpose of this meeting? Over the years, I have given my card to so many people at networking events, only to get that email or call the very afternoon or the next morning. "Hey, can we meet for coffee?" Or, "Here's my weekly newsletter, hope you like it."

In the beginning, I never asked the question, "why?" Suddenly, I found myself at a Starbucks listening to sales pitch after sales pitch. Use me, buy from me, invest in me. No, I don't know you, and now I don't want to! Now I hesitate before giving out my card unless I see a reason. It may be to meet just to get to know each other, or to see if there might be a reason to do business together. These types of bilateral meetings can be very productive. Just ask yourself before you make that call whether there's something in it for both of you or if there's value in the meeting.

Close talkers: Oh, no! Most people like their personal space. Respecting that is just common courtesy toward others. But there are those who just don't get it. I take a step back, and they step forward. Another step back and still they follow. Please learn to give people their personal space. We do not need to smell what you ate for breakfast today, or even worse yesterday. I have spoken to many people about this, and what they say is never polite. Business connections may be over before they have the chance to begin! Feel out the people you are speaking to. If he or she is moving back, stay where you are. Some people would rather have a bit of space while networking. You should at least have a pocket full of mints and use them.

Sellers: "Buy my stuff, now." "You need my stuff, buy it." "You need my product, buy it now!" They have no idea how this approach will harm their message. Never do the hard sell, because again, it may end the relationship before it begins. I may or may not need your product, but that will come in time. Do not rush the sale. Dr. Misner has a great line about this; he calls it, "Premature solicitation".

Some deals are about the chemistry or relationship between people, rather than the cost of the product. Take the time to listen to what their needs are and if you or your company have a solution, then present it, but not with a hard sell. Speak from knowledge you have on the subject and how you can help with an issue. You should be discussing the type of person you can help with your services. It's fine to ask for introductions to people they know who can use your services vs. selling to the networker. Remember, if they need or want more information they will ask. Then you can approach them about the sale.

Takers: Those at events who only want to leave with something they have not earned, but will settle for a big stack of business cards. They feel this will make the event worth their while. In truth, this type of person leaves with less than he or she arrived with. The person who comes with an open mind and a goal to meet new people and help others will be the actual winner at the event. "What can you do for me?" never really works. In fact, the message is so wrong it will often work against you and have the opposite effect. Who wants to be added to yet another email list or be harassed for a coffee meeting? People like this are the type of people I will never have any interest in helping. Bad karma!

Are you with me? You know those individuals who are not paying attention. These are the people who are looking over your shoulder to see if there is someone better to speak to. They are scanning the room for a better connection. Maybe they know who they are looking for, or it could be they see a well dressed person, and therefore that must be a better contact. Don't be that person. What does this say about *Your Message*? You've entered a conversation; be in that moment. This concept is so essential at networking events. People want to know you're listening and engaged in the conversation. You should never be thinking about who else is in the room. Looking over one's shoulder is a sign of pure disrespect. If you get caught in a conversation you don't want to be in because they are selling or just not speaking in your disc style, be polite. Let them finish, thank them, ask for a card and move on, but do not look around them into the crowd. You never know who they know, and you don't want to get a reputation for being the looker.

Interrupters: Cell phones, smart watches, texts, emails, calls, most of us will not do business with networkers who cannot give us undivided attention for a few minutes at an event. There are new electronics to distract us all the time. An earpiece that can read our messages to us, smartwatches that show us emails, texts, even pictures. These are a new set of distractions to interfere with our conversations. Turn them off! Give everyone your undivided attention. Even when the person you are speaking with may not be your optimal networking partner, don't look at the electronics. As discussed in the last section, you may find yourself looking to get away but keep the focus, be polite, then move on. However, before you dismiss the person, do you know who he or she knows? We all find ourselves in an uncomfortable situation every now and again, but stick with it, don't look to your electronics for freedom. Politely end the encounter and then move to the next contact.

Trade show collectors: These are the people who attend trade shows and think it is all about them. They feel these events are filled with business owners and salespeople who want to speak to them and buy their services. They travel the show trying to collect all the vendors' cards and speak to those behind the tables. Why are the vendors at these events? Why did these vendors pay for their tables or space? What are their goals or expectations for these networking events?

People who pay for booths or tables do not want a visitor to sell to them. What does *Your Message* look like if you go to a booth and stand in front preventing potential clients from reaching their destination? What does the vendor think about you and *Your Message*? Think about where you are; your goal should not be to create bad feelings. Stroll the show, and as you collect cards, ask if you can call in the future. This sends the right message.

The Collector and Blaster: These people go to networking events and try to collect as many business cards as they can. There is no good reason other than to obtain them. Many times, if you go to their offices you will find bags of cards, sometimes with labels going back months or years. Why? Two main reasons: they think they will contact them and never look at the cards again, or they blast out emails about their business. What does this say about *Your Message?* How many emails do you get per day? How many try to sell something or sign you up for a service? When I was a travel agent, before I understood the nuance of networking, I was a bag collector. I had a large stack of cards in labeled plastic bags. The upside is I was the person who never did a thing with those business cards instead of soliciting. Stay away from this behavior because it never reflects well on the person doing it or the business represented.

Name badges are also part of *Your Message.* Why do we wear name badges at networking events? When asked this question most people will reply, "So everyone knows my name." This answer is true, but not entirely. The reason is more about making people feel comfortable at these events. When we introduce ourselves, it is the first few words spoken and the hardest to remember. This is the reason we wear name badges. Most of us will admit it takes a few meetings and introductions to make a name stick to a face. Your name should be as large as you can fit it on the supplied materials. Some master networkers will create a personal name badge that will set them apart from the people in the room who are wearing the provided one.

Handouts and promotional products: These materials should be limited or nonexistent at networking events. You've seen them, and I admit that I was once one of the offenders. I would go to events when I was a travel agent and hand out my magazine to everyone I could convince to take it. This behavior was a mistake from which I had to learn a hard lesson. When you see the "take my stuff" networker, we tend to be polite and take it, or maybe not and then look for the first place to deposit it. Ok, toss it. There are only a few types of events in which you should use handouts or take away materials. Trade shows and events at which you are the keynote speaker or sponsor are the two that come to mind. It can damage *Your Message* if you are pushing your stuff on people. Trade shows, for example, would be the correct networking event to use these types of materials. Those who want it will take it. Some closed contact networking events have a dedicated table for such materials.

How do you stand when speaking to others at networking events? We may not think about this, but it is important. We form groups in open networking settings. How does it look to others? Can I get into the conversation? Am I wanted in this discussion, or is it a closed or private conversation?

When someone enters a room full of networkers, especially if they are new to the networking community and looking for someone to speak to, what do they see? The first thing they encounter is your body language and your appearance. We have already talked about your appearance, so let's look at body language. The first part is how you stand. Let's say there are two people squared off face to face. Does this create a warm and inviting feeling? What message is this sending? They will look for other people to network with instead of you or your group. This concept holds true for all size groups, three, four or a larger group. If you are four networkers and the ring is closed, probably no one else will try to step into this group. This networking concept is known as "open twos and threes." Now, if you are standing at a 90 degree angle to each other it will allow for a third person to feel good about walking over and starting or entering your conversation.

If you are in a group of three again stand in a "U" shape to allow others to join in your conversation.

Next is your general position. How are your arms, folded across your chest or open and welcoming? What does all this say about *Your Message*? Make sure you look open to speaking to others. That's the correct message.

In summary, think about *Your Message* as soon as you decide to attend an event. To become productive at outside events, you must have a goal before you attend. What type of event is it? What do you want to get from this event? Next, you will need to prepare for the event. Think about all the aspects and how your behavior will affect *Your Message*. Below is a quick checklist for you to think about as you plan your networking.

What will *Your Message* be? Don't forget to follow up on anything you say or promise at every event.

Action items:

- ✓ Why am I going?
- ✓ What is my goal?
- ✓ Do I need to register?
- ✓ What should I wear?
- ✓ Is there a cost? Do I need to bring cash, or will they accept a check?
- ✓ What time do I need to be there and how long will I stay?
- ✓ Should I invite a friend or associate to this event?
- ✓ Do I have enough business cards?
- ✓ Do I need any other materials? Do not forget a pen and something to take notes with.

CHAPTER 14

How you generate new clients, or not

Maybe you have not thought about all the different methods available to your business to generate new clients and how they affect *Your Message*. They do! Throwing a plastic sandwich bag with a quarter sheet of cut up paper with your contact information and a few small rocks to hold it in place on my driveway certainly sets the tone for *Your Message*. Every year I get several of these bags in my driveway or my front lawn. I guess they must pick up a few clients, but is this the type of business you are looking for? To me, this puts out a message of cheap, cheap, cheap. I would never use a business whose message was wrapped in a plastic bag with some rocks. Do they have insurance, are they registered as a business? Do they pay tax on their revenue? These are some of the questions that come to mind when I see the plastic bags.

Mailers: I know some studies state you need six touches before a client knows who you are and will use your company. The six-touch rule states a client will not use your business until he or she hears from your company at least six times. Letters, emails, phone calls, postcards and so on. I will also tell you that a lot of us at that point, are so sick of your multiple touches that we have now put you on our "never do business with them" blacklist. Many times, we will never use your company due to what I call "the annoyance factor."

Door hangers: There is good and bad with this approach. If you are really doing work on the street and you have a lawn sign on the client's property, then those techniques can be helpful and can boost your credibility. However, if you are just going door to door and papering all the homes on the street, and you have not done any local work, it may have a different effect.

Bothering me at night: Don't we all hate this? A knock on your door… you know nothing good will come from it, but they keep knocking. You get up and open the door. There he is, a low paid sales rep from some construction company. He proceeds to tell you how his company is doing all this work in your neighborhood, and since they are already working on your street, he would like to offer you a free estimate of work they feel your house needs. I love when they tell me I need new windows. Really? It's dark, how would you have any idea what my windows need? What is your experience in the industry of window replacement? This person looks like he is not even 18 years old yet? What if, as in my case, I want to keep my original 160 year old windows? Now back to their lack of creditability. Why have I not seen any lawn signs or even a truck with their name on it? I think we all know!

A few years back, just after I had replaced the second story windows in my house, it happened to me. The salesperson tells me how his windows will make my home warmer. I say to him, "I just replaced them, and I hope after a few months in my house they would still be in good shape." He tells me they are replacing the windows of some homes on my street. My question, "really, tell me who?" Well, that would be confidential. Again, I am good. Please leave, NOW.

Phone calls by marketing companies: I guess people must fall for the deals, but I tend never to do business with one I know nothing about. They call and call and call. Night after night after night until you finally you pick up and tell them you don't need their services, and then they call again. I get so many phone calls about health insurance. "I am calling on behalf of XYZ health insurance. We will have a representative in your area speaking to your neighbors. Would you like to meet with him?" Do you think I am going to fall for that?

Social media: Do you think asking me to "like" your page over and over and over again will lure me to be your client? I understand your need to have the most followers, but you need to respect my rights to be on social media without being harassed by you or your team to like your page. It's appropriate to ask once, but then stop. It is the equivalent of in the past we would get numerous phone calls on our landlines to buy or sign up for some product or service.

Networking can be a disaster if not done correctly. I made so many mistakes at networking events before I was enlightened. When I first became a travel agent, I fell victim to the views of others. I will share two stories of failure. First, when my wife and I were in Fort Lauderdale taking classes to gain our travel agent license, we were told of a restaurant in Miami that would send a limousine to pick us up, and at the end of the night return us to the hotel. Sounds good, so we called and booked the limo. Once in the limo we were sitting with eight other people. I thought, "golden opportunity". Wrong. I passed out my card and wanted to tell them about my company, "It's easy to remember!" I said. "If you can remember Fun On The Waves travel, I can book your vacation!" The issue was they didn't care. They were all on their way to Miami looking for a great night and great food. They didn't care about me. Thinking back on that night, they looked bothered, and guess what? None of them ever contacted me.

A few months after I started the travel agency, I joined the Main Line Chamber of Commerce. They had an event every month called Networking at Noon. One hundred or so business people at the same event, golden opportunity to promote my new travel agency. Boy was I wrong. I made two mistakes. There was a double sided buffet, and I stood at the end of the line and spoke to each person and gave my card. Everyone took it, even though none of them wanted it. What did they want? To eat, to network, not to be sold to. Almost all of them took the card, and almost all of them tossed it on the food collection tray, or just left them on the tables.

I attended another Networking at Noon event a few months later and I had just printed a travel magazine. How great! It even had a coupon to enter for a raffle for a free cruise. I walked around and attempted to give them away. Some people took them; others said no. I put some of them on the tables. How many clients did I get? In three years with the chamber, I booked two trips and quoted five. The revenue did not even cover the cost of my membership and the entrance fees to the events. I would have had better success if I realized that I needed to build relationships not push people to use me.

Print advertising: I am amazed how many letters I get from certain industries attempting to get me to call for a free quote. In my area, we get inundated with letters from real estate companies and insurance agencies. I get biweekly letters from a certain insurance company. They try to fool me with blank white envelopes with no return address. I get one from a company trying to buy my house. They send postcards stating, "Termination Warning." They are going to remove their offer if I don't let them buy my house! This type of threat tactic will not work. If I want to sell my house I will.

Now, I understand there are many people who will tell you about best practices in marketing such as the six-touch rule and the three-foot rule of business cards, but do they work in today's world? Reminder: The three-foot rule is that everyone within three feet of you at all times should have your business card and know what you can do for them. How many clients do you get vs. how many people you will alienate?

Be respectful and learn your target market. I am the vice-chair of the BNI Foundation and I want to get information into the hands of my donors. How many times should I contact then? How should I contact them? I was not sure, so I sent out a survey and asked them. Well it turns out they want email once a quarter. Now I understand my target market. I would tell you to reach out and ask, then decide what is the best way to reach that market, and above all, think about what *Your Message* looks like to them as the receiving party, not to you.

So, what should you do? How do you grow your client base? There are many options available to us, but what will work for you depends on your business and the type of clients you want.

I remember many times when I was running the travel agencies, people would say to me that travel agents are a dying breed. Who needs one when we have the internet? I would say the internet is the best source of high end clients. They search and search and find there is so much information it makes their heads spin. Once they have had their fill, they call a travel agent for help. Those who want the lowest price are not who I want for clients.

Some avenues, like BNI, will work for almost every business. Look at these in your target market. Think about how you received their information and how THEY will want to be approached. A balanced approach works best. It is just like disc assessment. If you received my email address because I clicked on your website and gave it to you, then most likely that is how you should market to me. Just remember to be respectful of my view of *Your Message.*

Action Items:

- ✓ Make a list of the different ways you advertise your business.
- ✓ Review each method to determine if any might offend the recipient.
- ✓ Contact a few clients and ask if they appreciate the contact.

CHAPTER 15
Estimates, why you need to give them

I was speaking to one of my business clients who is a plumber. He was having issues handling referrals and estimates. I asked, "What do you do when you receive a referral?" His answer was shocking! He said, "Most of the time I put them in my glove compartment until business is slow. Then I will pull them out and make the call." What does it say about *Your Message* when you don't follow up on personal referrals? Why do business people not return calls or give estimates?

What do unhappy clients do? They talk! Who do you tell when a business person gets it wrong? How long do they tell their story? *Forever!* Then they call their estate planning attorney and put the story in their will, so the next two generations can continue to tell the story about the company who did it wrong! Think carefully about how not returning a call will affect *Your Message.*

I was working with a client who came to me for help in closing his sales calls. He had plenty of referrals, but he was not closing many of them. So, I started by asking a few questions. When you receive a referral from whoever, wherever, what do you do? His answer was, "It depends on how busy I am." Wrong! I asked what is the time between receiving the referral and contact? Again "It depends." Wrong! What about the time between your visit to the client's project and the time you give the estimate? His answer, "It all depends." Wrong, Wrong, Wrong!

This issue is, unfortunately, prevalent with contractors, but it is by no means limited to them. Almost any business that gives quotes or estimates can fall victim to this trap. The trap is thinking it is ok to make people wait. Guess what? They don't need to wait, since there are so many businesses who do what you do.

You receive a referral. Now what? Do you need to set up an appointment? Make a call? What's next? Do you have a system? Do you follow it? I have heard so many sad stories about poor business practices, however, a lot of them come from the contracting or trade industries. Having owned and operated an electrical contracting business for over 25 years, I listened to so many people tell me stories about contractors who call, come out to see the job, and then there is no follow up. The homeowner calls leaves a message, waits and then gets angry. Business people need to realize the client took the time to meet with you; you took the time to look at the work and then the client presumed you wanted the work. Right? Why would you invest your time looking at a job and then not follow up with an estimate or at least call the client to tell them you do NOT want the work?

I have worked with many business people, owners, sales representatives and contractors and many of them seem to have the same disease, a lack of consistency in estimates and timelines.

You need a system, one that will allow you to track and hold yourself accountable for your actions. Always look at yourself through the eyes of your clients. How long would **you** wait? Once you receive the referral, contact should be the same day or a least within 24 hours.

Once you gather the appropriate information, make sure you get the estimate to the client either the same day or, again, within 24 hours. If you need time to write up your estimate, make a phone call and explain you need more time!

There are many systems you can buy to help you manage your estimates and contacts with your clients. If you do not have a system in place, get one!

Action items:

- ✓ Analyze your estimate system.
- ✓ Do you track the time between contact by the client and your meeting?
- ✓ Do you track the time from the meeting until you deliver the estimate?
- ✓ Do you track the time from the estimate until you check back with the client?

CHAPTER 16

Collecting your money is part of *Your Message*

Sometimes people might get behind and owe you money. They may not pay promptly, or just flat out refuse to pay. The issue will arise in every business, but if you get angry, and you will, it may affect *Your Message*. Leaving angry or threatening messages, screaming at your clients is never the answer.

When I was an electrician I worked on a job with a painter who, at the end of the job, demanded his money. The homeowner told him she could not pay his bill, since her husband handled bill paying. He got mad and raised his voice to her. She told him that demanding his money was not helping. He then began to scream and yell at her, demanding she give him a check.

Having run several businesses over the past 30 plus years, I think I have listened to just about every possible variation of excuses that are out there. I have come to understand that people can give the most astounding excuses and not realize that they are not even believable! I also understand the anger of business owners as they listen to stories like, "My husband has the checkbook". It was a shock to me that you wanted to get paid. Ok, I understand your family only has one checkbook and your husband carries it with him at all times.

I get it. We all hate when people lie to our faces. However, it is part doing business, whether we like it or not. I asked the painter to step outside, and he agreed he would return in the morning to meet with her husband and collect the money.

What message was this business owner sending? My first thought is that he has no money, and he could not pay his bills, and that is why he's angry. I understand; you had an agreement and they broke it and now they won't pay so what should I do? I know I am going to lose my temper and threaten him with legal action. I will come back each day and demand payment. I will tell his neighbors. All bad ideas. If you want to collect payment at the end completion of the work, make sure the client has a clear understanding of the payment terms.

If *Your Message* is to be clear, you need to set expectations from the beginning. Always have an explicit contract that spells out the terms of the product or service. It does not need to be a long winded and complicated contract, just a clear set of expectations. I agree to provide this, and you agree to pay that in this time frame. You can even include terms of past due or late payments. Just check with the local laws, since they vary from state to state.

I met a contractor at a networking event. He said he was no longer closing the jobs like he did in the past. He asked me if I would review his contract and I agreed to do so. We went to his truck and he gave me a blank contract. He asked me what I thought. In my head, I thought Wow, if I received this the deal would be over instantly! His basic contract was 18 pages long and he was wonder why he was having trouble closing the deal with his clients! Just a basic agreement in simple language with all terms spelled out is all you need.

Never damage *Your Message* by losing your temper or making demands that have no teeth. Find out the why. What is the reason they have decided not to follow the terms of the agreement? Is there something that they are not satisfied with? Lashing out only gives them reason to delay and stall your payment.

Think about the process from the customer's eyes. If the terms are clear from the start, there will be far fewer issues with payment. Again, make sure you have a clear contract with easy to read terms. Make sure you do not do extra work or provide extra services until you have a change order completed and signed by all parties, and in which they agree to amend the original contract and pay the additional amount. If extra services are requested, always get it in writing as an addendum or a new agreement. Make certain the client has a copy and that they understand the scope of the work before you begin.

Many years ago, I was on a very large electrical job. I had a contract and payment plan terms. I had worked for this family for over 15 years. I had completed multi-million dollar construction projects for them. There was never an issue; I trusted them! My first mistake.

Not all family members and friends are as trustworthy as those they refer. The house was coming along, and as with any remodeling job with a large addition, things are constantly evolving. Cut wires, old wiring discovered in the way of the construction or adding a light here or a cable outlet there. Everything was going well. I had turned in multiple change orders, 73 of them, to give you the actual numbers. When the job was done, all appeared to be fine and the family was happy with the work. Not a single issue ensued on the final punch list. Then I turned in the bill for the extras. The general contractor asked, "What extras?" My reply, "I turned in the change orders and you signed them." His response was, "Do you have the homeowner's signature on any of them?" Well, I knew now that I was in trouble! I then went to the homeowner who wasn't giving in. I spoke to his father, who was a client for 20 years. He said, "I don't get into my children's business." When I went to their legal counsel regarding this they informed me that they could tie me up in court and even if I won a judgment I would need to collect and that would be another battle.

The result was I was out tens of thousands of dollars, and I learned a valuable business lesson. Get everything in writing with clear terms and don't do any work until this step is completed! I had very few options. I kept my cool and moved on. I could have done several things, but none would have helped my message in the community.

Let's talk about destroying *Your Message* through a simple email. This was an attempt by an office manager to collect money through an email. I was out to breakfast with one of my daughters when she began to tell me a story of an issue with a CSA (Community Supported Agriculture). This is a community based company that relies on having an excellent local message to promote their business. They had a new employee who decided to send out an email, which began, "**We have passed the final payment due date of Feb 6, 2016, and your account has a past due balance.** As stipulated in the CSA agreement all payments are expected by the final date of the contract. The agreement you signed at the beginning of the season is a binding contract in which you agreed to support our regional farmers for this season." On and on it went, and it threatened to file an action on those who did not settle their debt.

When you read this, you might think the CSA had every right to send this email. This employee, however, was wrong to do so since the contract terms were not exactly as she quoted. But you would not know that by reading her email. The more significant issue was the tone of the message and a change in the way the CSA did business evidenced by sending out a threatening message and thereby alienating their clientele.

In the past, they would always remind members of the amounts due on their accounts when they picked up their produce. Another major problem with her message, which could have become costly or even a legal issue for the owners, was that the sender listed over 50 names in the "cc" area of the email. Now all those people were branded as slow pay or bad customers to everyone on the list!

Always, always use the "bcc" section when listing more than one person or business name in a group email, no matter what the topic is. If one of these people on the list wanted to blast a mass response, it was as easy as "reply all." What if someone on that list decided to respond with a nasty reply calling for everyone to stop using their company? The CSA just gave them their client list all in one convenient location.

When it does go wrong, and it will, keep your cool and try to resolve it in a friendly manner. This will allow you to keep *Your Message* untarnished. Yelling and threatening is never the way to address an issue. Writing emails that are perceived as a threat will never endear you or your company to your clients. Never start off with, "I will sue you, you will lose and owe me even more money." This threat will most often not work. Trust me. Been there; done that. Even if you win, it is hard to collect. The court system is not your friend, even if you did everything right!

When I was an electrician, I had a client I had worked for many times. She lived in a very large, eight bedroom, six bathroom house in Gladwyne Pa. I am not sure of the value, but it had to be in the millions! I put a set of flexible ground lights around her patio, because her son kept breaking the lights that were initially installed. The job went very well and she was happy and said she would mail the payment to me, just as she had done in the past. When I opened the envelope, it was short $700.00. There was no reason listed. I called her several times with no reply. I sent another invoice and again there was no reply. I sent certified letters and invoices. Nothing. So, I filed in small claims court. Guess what? The judge ruled I had made enough money and she was just a single parent making ends meet. Really, and she was living in a house worth millions? The courts are not always your friend!

Another quick story about our legal system. A business associate, and a good friend who has outstanding contracts and always collects deposits, installed an air conditioning system for a general contractor in Philadelphia. When it came to the final payment, the general contractor began to stall with excuses. "The owner has not paid me yet." "The work you did is not exactly how we laid it out," and so on. All were lies. The payment due was $2,800.00. After many attempts, his partner said, "Let's just sue him. So, they called the contractor and stated their intentions. The contractor offered $1000.00 to settle. They should have taken the deal. On to court they went. The judge ruled in their favor, and as they were leaving the courthouse feeling good, the partner who insisted they not take the settlement asked the lawyer, "When do we get our check?" The lawyer laughed, "Well that is a different story. We have a judgment; now you need to try to collect it." So, to wrap up this story, they were out the $2800, plus the filing fees and legal fees. Sometimes it is just better to take the settlement and call it a day!

Protect yourself with proper paperwork and clear terms and get money up front to mitigate the loss in the event that something does go wrong. All that said, I also understand sometimes there is nothing you can do if the client is just not a good person. This does not mean you should drop to their level. Always keep *Your Message* as professional as possible. Remember, in today's world people can post on social media sites any variety of negative remarks, even if they're not true. Once that message is out, there it lives forever and that will be your legacy. Always take the higher road, try to resolve any issues, and then hire a good law firm or collection company to do the ugly work and collect your money.

Action items:

- ✓ Make sure you get a deposit and have the terms of payment described in detail on your contracts.
- ✓ Instead of getting angry, ask questions, find out what went wrong, and fix it. This costs far less than a lawyer!

CHAPTER 17

OH NO, What just happened

An accurate measure of *Your Message* is how you react to, and resolve issues or problems when things go wrong. And they will go wrong! No company will ever have 100% satisfaction, and if it does it will be short lived. People, in general, will find reasons to create issues, even though sometimes the issue is the client. What you do about it and how you do it is an explicit representation of *Your Message*. If, and when a client calls with a problem or concern over work that was done, never turn it around and make it his or her problem, even if he or she is at fault.

For example, a client calls to tell you the work that was done in the house six months ago is not holding up. The cement walkway leading up to the front door from the driveway has cracked and needs to be replaced or fixed. The client is upset, since he or she paid a lot of money to remodel the front of the house, and expected a level of quality from the contractor. He or she is looking to you for a solution, not a story. My mother had just such an issue. The reply from the contractor was, "Well, cement can sometimes crack." The long winded story began... there are so many reasons that cement can crack. The list of possibilities went on even though all she wanted to hear was, "I will fix it". He continued, "It is an old house, and sometimes there is a bit of settlement after the work is completed;

maybe the cement was defective; maybe it was too cold." The work was completed in August in Pennsylvania! "Someone in your family must have walked on it before it was finished setting, and there may have been an air pocket in the stone." On and on he went. "I will come out sometime when it is convenient for me and look at it. I might be able to fix it but it may need to be redone, and there may be an additional cost."

Now, what is the client, in this case my mother, thinking? I know just what she was thinking. She immediately got angry, and the more he talked, the angrier she got! How did this message sound to her? It seemed to be everyone's fault but his.

I had sent the contractor to do the work, and there was this issue of a few cracks in the front walkway. When I called the contractor, he had two options. One was to take responsibility and offer to fix the walkway as soon as a time could be arranged, or he could have listed all the possible reasons why it was not his fault. I would have been much happier if he had reacted with the first response. Unfortunately, I received the second. Guess who will not get the opportunity to do more work for me, my family, or any other person I ever run into in need of cement work? What was the message?

I was just one year into my career as a travel agent. I booked my first group cruise with thirty six people and seventeen cabins. I could see the results in my head and the jump in my client base. They would all be so happy; they would tell all their friends about me and my excellent customer service. The bus picked them up in Philadelphia and delivered them to Cape Liberty, NJ. (For those of you who know the area it was the old Bayonne port. If you know the area you will get the joke. For the rest of you it was an old port mostly used for shipping containers. The area was considered a high crime area and by no means a luxury cruise port! The cruise lines just changed the name). Off they went! Yay, my first group! I sent gifts to the cabins: champagne and chocolate covered strawberries for the adults, milk and chocolate covered cookies for the kids. There was a private party on the first night with drinks and hot appetizers. What could go wrong?

Then they came back and began to call. Oh, no. One day into the trip one of the three propellers fell off! The cruise line decided to continue the cruise but would cut two of the four ports of call. What did the cruise line do to make the passengers feel better about their vacation? They gave them all the port charges back, $12.98 for each passenger. If you have been on a cruise, you understand that does not even cover the cost of a single drink!

What a disaster; I was getting calls every day. They were all angry, not so much with me, but in general about how they were all treated. It was my good luck to have just taken a course on customer service. I learned the most valuable lesson. Listen, listen, listen, and then listen some more. People want to know you care. When they were done venting, I asked a simple question. What can we do together to solve this problem? The answer they gave me was simple, "I have no idea, what do you think?" My answer was, "Why don't you write me a letter, and I will put them all together and send them to the district sales manager for the cruise line. What a great idea! I received four letters from the eighteen phone calls I received. The cruise line did not do anything to help, but the moral is people just want to be heard.

What sets the good companies apart from the bad, and the great companies from the good, is how they handle complaints and the issues that will arise. Does it matter whose fault it is? What matters is how the client feels and how you respond. How does *Your Message* look to the client, not to you? What does your response say about you, as the representative of the business?

So, what is the correct way to deal with problems and issues, and how can *Your Message* be viewed as a positive one when the client is upset? The best way to start is to listen, then, listen some more, followed by a bit of listening. People want you to hear them and their pain. Sometimes all they want is for you to listen. Then, how about a response that starts with, "I am so sorry you are having an issue," or "What can we do to make it right for you?" You can use the Feel Felt Found process. After they are done telling you their issue you can say, "I understand how you feel, others have felt that way, we have found the best way to solve this is..." In the case of my mother's cement, he could have said, "I do not know what caused this to happen, but I will find out and get it fixed as soon as possible. When can I come out to take a look?" That would have created a positive message, unlike what he did. His response was a negative message.

You and *Your Message* will always be judged by how you handle ensuing problems and how you receive and manage complaints.

The next time a client has an issue, before you respond, make sure you listen and then ask questions. Tell me what the issue is? If you are not sure, ask how you can help. Make sure *Your Message* is a positive and productive one that leaves your clients telling people how great you handled the situation.

Action items:

- ✓ Make sure you have a thought out process for when things go wrong.
- ✓ Always look into the issue from the eyes of your client before you react.

CHAPTER 18

Your employees and subcontractors are you

Working with many types of business owners, we have to address the problematic issue of those we surround ourselves with. We want and need to grow our businesses, and as we do, we need to build our staff to support this growth. Who you invite to be on your team has a direct impact on the quality of *Your Message*.

Think about the last time you had a contractor to your house. How did he or she look? How did he or she sound? Does he or she smell like cigarettes? Did they respect your home and your wishes? Doors closed, lights off, and no smoking near your front door? Did your dog get out, did you find his or her trash in your trash cans, or worse yet left around your property? Did you walk out front and see cigarette butts tossed around the sidewalk?

Think about when you last called your doctor's office. Was the staff polite and accommodating? Did they treat you with respect and give you their full attention? Or did they put you on hold with a quick "hold please" followed by ten minutes of bad music? Who does the music appeal to? Is it some canned music that you, the owner, has never heard? Often the staff is not focused on the client, but on whatever is in front of them at the time. A patient, paperwork, chatting with another employee and none of these will represent

Your Message in a positive light. Ultimately, I complained about my doctors' staff and nothing was done. I finally changed doctors, I can't be the only one!

A while back, I called a local business owner I knew, who owned a bicycle shop. I had met another business person at an event who had a product that could save the owner thousands of dollars per year. It was a new type of degreaser. I tried to set up a call. The phone rang.

"Hello, The Smith Bike shop, this is Tom."

"I am calling to speak to George, is he in?"

"No, he will be back this afternoon; can you call back?"

Well, ok! Four hours later I call again,

"Hello, this is Smith Bike Shop, John speaking."

Again, I say, "I am calling to speak with George, is he in?"

"No, he will be back later. Can I help you?"

"No thanks," I say, "I need to talk to George."

"Well can you call back?" (Again, with the call back).

"Can I leave a message?"

"Well, hold on… Ok, who are you?"

I leave my information and thank him for his help. Did I get a callback? Did George get the message? Who knows? I do know he never called me back, and I will never call there again. What if I were a client who wanted to buy a new high end bike? Business lost.

This part of *Your Message* is entirely under your control. You decide who represents *Your Message*. Often this decision becomes more about perceived profits than the view or feelings of your clients. I know that some businesses will hire and keep people around just because they will do the necessary work at the lowest cost, and therefore increase the short range profits. But the long range picture is a loss of profits. The amount of missed or lost business will far outweigh the short range savings. So, I would tell you that you need to pay enough money per hour, within the going rate of your profession to get and retain quality employees. It is also important to train them to operate in the fashion that will create a quality message to your clients.

Some of the people we hire are not the happiest of people. Maybe a raise and a mirror put by the phone or on their desks would help. Teach them that a smile can be seen through the phone. We know it can be seen in person. You should view *Your Message* through the eyes of your clients. Does your team treat your clients the way you would want to be treated? How do you know?

Action item:

- ✓ Ask your clients how they feel they are treated by your staff? Do they feel valued?
- ✓ Have a third party call your clients after each appointment or service call and ask for feedback.

CHAPTER 19

Time for self evaluation, the hard part

It is always hard to look at yourself and be honest about what you see. It is like proofreading your own document. You can read it over and over and still not see the misspelled word. Our mind knows what should be there and tricks us into seeing it. Our view may not be what is really there. You may have deceived yourself into thinking you are doing things in *Your Message* that you are not. *Your Message* might be "misspelled."

We are worried about how others view us in so many ways, but not when it comes to our business. Always remember perception is a reality. It is the other's, not yours, and their perspective is their reality.

Look at Facebook and other forms of social media; we do things to attract "likes." Go to a popular nightclub and look at the people, they are all dressed to draw attention. Go down to the shore and do some people watching. Watch those who are parading down by the water's edge. Look at how they dress. So why, when it comes to our businesses, do we stop thinking about how others will view us, and only think about ourselves?

It's time to do a little self evaluation. This can be challenging, since any exercise that requires you to look at *Your Message* through the eyes of others is undoubtedly not going to be easy. You will need to examine all the individual parts we have discussed in each chapter, because together they make up the big picture of *Your Message*.

To have a truly successful business, you need to think of others first and what is important to them. You must make it easy for people to do business with you.

Being great at a few parts of *Your Message* will not be enough to keep you on top of your competitors in the business world. When I was running my electrical contracting business, I was skilled at running the jobs. I was an artist as an electrician. But I was not very gifted on the business side, running the back end of the business. I made more money, and things ran much more smoothly when I had only two or three employees and could control my message. Once I grew the business and had eleven on staff, things began to fall apart. I slipped on the follow up and the paperwork got away from me. I had a few options, and I went with the easy and smart choice for me at the time, to cut back the business. In the long run, I should have taken a different path. I should have looked in from the outside to see what part of my message needed work and fixed it. I should have asked for help!

The issue that I had to deal with was that no one told me I was slipping; they just went elsewhere for the work.

I thought everything was just fine, but then the business fell off. The client calls slowed down; I stopped getting the jobs I used to. It is always so much easier to blame everything on others and outside influences. I thought, the client should have understood I was busy, and they should have been able to wait for the estimate. They should have understood that I did not scratch their table; it must have been there before my men started the job! I could list all the things I could have done better. I never looked into what was really going on with the process of my business until it was out of control. So, when you take a truly reflective look, you will find that almost all downfalls point back to your flawed decisions. Don't be the me then; be the me now! I never get offended when I hear what others think of my business.

Guiding others to look within themselves is often a challenging and complicating task. The picture is never what they think it is or hope it to be. People get very defensive when they are confronted with the harsh reality of the truth that is their message viewed from their client's eyes. We all need to look in the mirror, even if we don't like what we see. We need to be honest with ourselves. Think about every aspect of *Your Message* from the eyes of your clients, or prospective clients.

When you reflect on it, the people who matter most are your clients, not you, once you understand this concept you can begin to have the opportunity to change.

All right now, let's get started! Get a sheet of paper and be truthful with yourself. Answer the following questions. You might even get one of your clients to help you, or maybe send the list of questions out like a survey. Once you have the replies, you can begin to make a difference in *Your Message*!

Go down the list below and think how others see *Your Message*. Review the entire experience, from the first contact until they get the thank you for the privilege of having them as a client. Could you do better? I bet you can. We can all do better no matter your level, you can rise to the next level and improve *Your Message*.

- ✓ How does your appearance look to others when you leave your house? From Dr. Ivan Misner, what do you look like from 12 feet? What do you look like from 12 inches?
- ✓ How do you sound when you speak to people?
- ✓ How do you sound on your phone?
- ✓ What voicemail response do your callers hear?
- ✓ How does your business card look? Who does it speak to? Pull it out and look it over.
- ✓ How do your other materials look?
- ✓ Open your website? Is it outdated? Could it be better? Does it work on a tablet, smart phone?
- ✓ Are you one of those who say and post too much on social media? What is the message you are sending? Does *Your Message* involve politics, religion, or social views that might upset your readers?
- ✓ Do you respond to your emails in a timely fashion, and are your responses clear to those who receive them?
- ✓ Do you communicate well?
- ✓ Follow up, follow up… are you following up quickly?
- ✓ Phone calls, emails, estimates, and quotes… How long do they take?
- ✓ When you are communicating with others, do you know who you are you speaking to? Remember there are four types of people. Can you figure out which is which?
- ✓ Outside events… Are you ready? Do you have a goal?
- ✓ Collecting money…Is it done professionally?
- ✓ To whom are you speaking, and do they understand you?

Review all the questions above, and then make a list of all the other facets of your business. There are things you can correct that are easy and some that will be more difficult. What are the easiest to fix that will make the largest and most profound changes to *Your Message?* What do you need to do to get to the next level? Remember to think as if you are a prospective or current client. Look through his or her eyes from his or her perspective, not yours. Next, wait a day or two and then look at it again. Let someone you trust look at your list and see if he or she agrees with your self assessment. Ask your clients; just be ready for their answers, and don't get upset with the feedback you receive. Use it to improve *Your Message.*

CHAPTER 20
Can you change, yes, I think you can

Yes, I am confident you can! Changing *Your Message* may be a continual work in progress and making simple changes will be more comfortable than you think! The real question is, do you want to put in the effort and thought into making *Your Message* a different, more productive positive one? Can you do what it takes to create meaningful change, or will this book just look pretty on the shelf with the others?

Understand the one primary theme of this book and you will be on the path to success. Always remember, it is not now, and never has been, about you. It is, and always will be, about those you encounter, or who come in contact with *Your Message*. If *Your Message* is about your ego, you will become your best customer and ultimately have few others.

Some business owners have had the privilege of having an honest encounter with someone willing to point out the thing that needed to be changed. But then what? How was it taken? You say, "Thanks for the information, I truly appreciate the input," but in your mind you are annoyed or even angry. "What nerve! How dare he or she tell me that, to criticize me?"

There are many ways to begin; you just need to take the first step. What is the easiest aspect of *Your Message* to change that will have the most significant impact on your clients? What can you do today?

It is all up to you! If you have been to any of my presentations, seminars, or training, you know I love the toolbox theory. I can give you a brand new toolbox. It will be filled with a wonderful set of shiny new tools. But I can't make you open the box and use the tools!

So, you bought this book, but what you actually bought was that shiny new toolbox. It's a vast new toolbox filled with informational essentials designed to make you think and help implement change in *Your Message*. Can you create the change needed to make a difference? It may take time, and if your existing message was off track, it will not change overnight. But everyone can improve.

If you are resistant or afraid to take the first step, it's all right. Download the checklist from my website (www.YourBusinessBasics.com), select one topic each week, and review what you are doing and how you are doing it. Go back and evaluate each piece of *Your Message*. You need to remember, reading this book cannot fix or change *Your Message*. Only you can create change, and only you can decide when or where to start.

So, what will you do? Will you look at *Your Message* from your clients' eyes, or will you continue to view it from yours? Will you ask for the insight of others and not be offended when told the truth, or sit back and wait to see what will happen next?

If you read the entire book, did you figure it out yet? No, let me help you.

Go back to the start and look through each chapter, but every place you see the "*Your Message*" change the words to *My Business*.

Maybe you feel you are already successful, and you may be, but could you be better? It's all up to YOU! No one can make you exert the effort needed to take *Your Message* to the next level. Change must come from within. Only YOU can make the changes.

Now get to it; don't wait. Every minute you waste thinking about it could cost you a client!

APPENDIX 1

Checklist of important areas of *Your Message* to review.

- ☐ How does your business card look? Who does it speak to? Pull it out and look it over.
- ☐ How do your other materials look?
- ☐ Open your website? Is it outdated? Could it be better? Does it work on a tablet, smart phone?
- ☐ Are you one of those who say and post too much on social media? What is the message you are sending? Does *Your Message* involve politics, religion, or social views that might upset your readers?
- ☐ Do you respond to your emails in a timely fashion, and are your responses clear to those who receive them?
- ☐ Do you communicate well?
- ☐ Follow up, follow up... are you following up quickly?
- ☐ Phone calls, emails, estimates, and quotes... How long do they take?
- ☐ When you are communicating with others, do you know who you are you speaking to? Remember there are four types of people. Can you figure out which is which?
- ☐ Outside events... Are you ready? Do you have a goal?
- ☐ Collecting money...Is it done professionally?
- ☐ To whom are you speaking, and do they understand you?
- ☐ How do you sound when you speak to people?
- ☐ How do you sound on your phone?
- ☐ What voicemail response do your callers hear?
- ☐ What do your clients think of your message?

Foundation

The BNI Foundation is a non-profit that supports charitable causes relating to children and education in countries where BNI is operating.

Started by Ivan and Beth Misner in 1998, the BNI Foundation has been supporting children and education in the United States and around the world by mobilizing resources to give kids everywhere a quality education. The focus of the Foundation is to change the trajectory of the youth of our community and help them find the path to productive and successful lives. For us, the mechanism to help with this shift is by investing our time, treasure, and talent to assist in education where we can.

BNI has a long, proud legacy of reaching in and helping out where schools have needed extra funding for specific projects not provided for by school districts or state funding. A pivotal factor of our philanthropic work was the creation of the Business Voices® initiative to provide even more to the schools with the greatest needs. Our initiative pairs members and concerned, engaged and motivated corporations, service clubs and community groups with schools and educational organizations to help them find the resources they need to have maximum impact on the kids of our communities.

To learn more about the Foundation or to make a donation, please visit www.BNIFoundation.org

ABOUT THE AUTHOR

David Kauffman is a business adviser, coach, and the Managing Director of BNI Delaware Valley Regions. He is the owner of Your Business Basics, a consulting firm specializing in business process. He helps business owners understand how their actions, or lack thereof, affect their business. David is a keynote speaker and corporate trainer. He currently supports the business development efforts of over 3200 business professionals.

David started in business over 30 years ago with his first company, Secured Monitoring Systems, followed by Jor-Dan Electric. Later, he sold the alarm company and began Kauffman Construction. He then transitioned out of construction into the travel business with Fun on the Waves Travel. Over the years, David became an expert in customer service, focusing on the concept that customers would have the best possible experience if we looked at each business from their eyes; what was important to them. He is still a travel agent, but now devotes his efforts to BNI, Delaware Valley Regions and his business coaching clients.

The BNI Foundation, which supports childhood education, is very important to David. The children of today, are the business owners of tomorrow. He is currently on the board of directors as the Vice-Chair.

David and his wife, Pam, have four adult children and three grandchildren. They reside near Philadelphia, Pennsylvania. David enjoys volunteering for animal rescue and developed and manages the adaptive aquatics program at the Haverford Area YMCA, teaching special needs children water safety and swim techniques. He spends his spare time biking, swimming, and working in his backyard, a certified wildlife habitat that includes a large koi pond.

As an entrepreneur and author, David brings a solid background to his work, helping companies build stronger relationships with their customers and improve the processes of running a profitable business.

For information on his availability, contact him at David@YourBusinesBasics.com.